MESSIAH TO THE MESSED UP

Because I'm a mess, you're a mess, and we all need a Messiah

By
SUE CIULLO

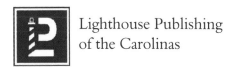

Lighthouse Publishing
of the Carolinas

MESSIAH TO THE MESSED UP BY SUE CIULLO
Published by Lighthouse Publishing of the Carolinas
2333 Barton Oaks Dr., Raleigh, NC, 27614

ISBN: 978-1-941103-16-6
Copyright © 2014 by Sue Ciullo
Cover design by Ted Ruybal, www.wisdomhousebooks.com
Interior design by Reality Info Systems, www.realityinfo.com

Available in print from your local bookstore, online, or from the publisher at:
www.lighthousepublishingofthecarolinas.com

For more information on this book and the author visit: www.sueciullo.com

Brought to you by the creative team at LighthousePublishingoftheCarolinas.com:
Denise Loock, Eddie Jones, Rowena Kuo, Meaghan Burnett, and Brian Cross

Library of Congress Cataloging-in-Publication Data
Ciullo, Sue.
Messiah to the Messed Up / Sue Ciullo 1st ed.

Printed in the United States of America

Praise for *Messiah to the Messed Up*

⁓∞⁓

If you have ever felt too messed up for Jesus to forgive or use you, read *Messiah to the Messed Up*. Author Sue Ciullo uses Scripture to introduce messed up characters that God forgives and uses in mighty ways. Before you give up, pick this book up!

~Dave Ferguson
Lead Pastor, Community Christian Church
Author of *Exponential*, *On the Verge*, and
Discover Your Mission Now

In her book, *Messiah to the Messed Up*, Sue Ciullo reminds all of us that we are indeed messed up. We've messed up in the past, and we will mess up in the future. But there is hope. While Christians believe Jesus was and is the long-promised Messiah of Israel, a careful look at the stories of His life reveal that He had a particular penchant for the messed up.

Jesus came to redeem all of us, including the messiest of us. Sue invites the reader to take a journey with this Jesus, the Messiah to the Messed Up. She invites us to experience the stories of Jesus found in the New Testament and rediscover the hope He brought to messy people in Israel and the hope He can bring to the messed up today.

Whether you have been studying the life of Jesus for years, or you are investigating His life for the first time, *Messiah to the Messed Up* will help you understand Jesus and His compassion for each of us.

~Patrick O'Connell
Director of NewThing

I've spent many years working with the Bible, from study notes to study guides to inspirational stories to devotional thoughts. Sometimes I wonder if anything new can be said. And then someone comes along with fresh eyes on the stories we know so well. Sue is one of those people.

In *Messiah to the Messed Up*, Sue draws us into the beloved gospel stories by looking at them with fresh insight and good study information. Then she offers up stories from her own life, illustrating her love for her Messiah and how He has worked in her life. You'll relate to her laughter, her joy, her grief, her repentance, her regret, and ultimately, her complete and total love for her Savior. And you'll be challenged to let that Messiah take whatever is messed up in your life and redeem it for His glory.

~Linda Taylor, M.A.
Editor on *The Life Application Study Bible*
Author of *Praying God's Promises for My Child*
and *Saints and Scoundrels of the Bible*

If you've always wanted to know more about Jesus, if you've longed to see Him more clearly, let Sue Ciullo reintroduce Him to you. *Messiah to the Messed Up* delivers a long look at Jesus through the lens of love.

See His love in the way He treated a whore or an outcast of society. Get a glimpse of it as it is acted out in the nitty-gritty of modern life. The beautiful message of *Messiah to the Messed Up* is that Jesus wants to touch each of our messed up lives and transform them with His love.

~Sharla Fritz
Author of *Divine Design* and *Bless These Lips*

Messiah to the Messed Up takes the stories of the Bible and relates them to real life and real time. Sue brings in her own stories to inspire us to receive the great gift of God's grace through Jesus. Never again should we assume that we have to clean up our act to come to God. He calls us just as we are and then challenges us to be transformed. An inspiring and practical book that will change lives.

~Janet McMahon
Community Life Director, Restore Community Church
Church Planter

Beautifully written, *Messiah to the Messed Up* will resonate with readers of today, giving fresh meaning and perspective to centuries-old biblical stories. A must read for those who know they've made mistakes and especially for those who think they haven't. We've all fallen from grace, we've all messed up, and we're all in need of a Messiah.

~Connie Cameron
Speaker and Author
Stories of Faith and Courage from Prison
God's Gentle Nudges
Co-founder, Set Free in Him Ministries

Dedication

To my son, Michael.

The moment I learned that I was carrying you,
I dropped to the floor in gratitude
to the Father who breathed you into my life.
I'm still grateful every day for the joy you bring to me.
I cherish in my heart the memories of your boyhood
and am so proud of the man you've become.

Acknowledgments

Until I became a writer, I'd always believed writing to be a solitary process. I know now that it is a team sport, and I have a multitude of team members to acknowledge for their contributions to this book.

The Write to Publish Conference in Wheaton, IL, gave me the resources I needed to pursue the promptings God gave me. My thanks to Lin Johnson, Jane Rubietta, and Joyce Ellis for their tireless efforts to give wings to new authors. Dr. Dennis Hensley is a genius, giving the keenest of insight and providing renewed direction to my writing. Jennifer Schuchmann understood my vision and gave me guidance to bring clarity to my renderings.

My Read Letters Critique Group turned my manuscript from one that I would be embarrassed to show to an editor to one that would demonstrate my promise as an author. My thanks to the women in this group who cared enough to tell me when I veered off course: Afton Rorvik, Linda Chafee Taylor, Sandi Stein, Linda McGee, Debbie Simler-Goff, Gail Ficken, and Jessica Keller Koschnitzky. Special thanks to my friend Sharla Fritz, who stuck with me from cover to cover and gave me personal guidance with some particularly difficult edits.

To my amazement, Ken Gire asked to read a copy of my manuscript. Ken is the maestro of Christian pathos writers, yet he took the time to critique my manuscript. Ken's contributions to this manuscript are enormous and have improved the book immensely. Ken is genuine, humble, and gracious. It is my great honor to have benefited from his talent and insight.

My small group at Community Christian Church eagerly embraced studying an earlier draft of my manuscript, a gesture that honored me deeply. Sincere thanks to Tim and Mary Yep, Jeff and Pam Haines, Lisa Reyes, Keith Kinton, Debbie Klocke, and Dave and Debbie Rubenstein. Special thanks to Debbie Rubenstein for being so enthused about the message of *Messiah to the Messed Up* that she committed to leading the book study for another small group. I am touched.

My siblings showed me their support from the start. Thanks to Ron Andersen, Marge Harrington, Judy Petersen, Tom Andersen, Jim Andersen, Janet Vrtis, and Laura Conlon for encouraging me along the way. I am particularly grateful for the overflowing enthusiasm and encouragement of my brother, John Andersen. I don't think a month went by in the past four years that John failed to call me for the express purpose of inquiring about my book or to offer advice or encouragement. John has been my biggest cheerleader throughout this project and my source of encouragement when I needed it most.

My dear friends Karen Gehse and Donna Ruehlmann each graciously opened up their homes to me while they were on vacation with their families so I would have a place to stay and to write in solitude. That seclusion resulted in some of my most productive work.

Sincere gratitude to my beta readers—Sue's Inside Team— who carefully read the proof copies of this book, scouring it for typos and grammatical errors. The contributions of these friends have made this a better book: Tracy Adams, Toni Behof, Paula Broughton, Connie Cameron, Stacey Ciullo-Ramos, Laura Conlon, Joanne DiNovo, Vicky Gerken, Sonya Karl, Doria Quintana, Carol Jensen Reda, Jane Shannon, Courtney Stasica, and Laina Wing.

My pastors at my beloved Community Christian Church have been enormously influential in my walk of faith. Tim Sutherland, Shawn Williams, and Dave Richa remain wonderful teaching pastors to me. Dave Ferguson is a visionary master. He has been instrumental in bringing me to the realization of the overpowering love of God. His influence planted in me the desire to write this book, that I may help people find their way back to God. Andy Stanley, of North Point Community Church in Alpharetta, GA, remains my "other" pastor. Although we've never met, Andy's teachings, via video and books, have made Jesus' message come alive for me.

Eddie Jones at Lighthouse Publishing of the Carolinas took an interest in the project that I described to him, gave me ideas to market my manuscript, and ultimately accepted the manuscript of this first-time author. Eddie is keenly focused on providing an avenue for Christian authors to bring their messages to readers eager to know Jesus better.

I am amazed at the tenacity and vigilance of my editor, Denise Loock. I have seen her strengthen the impact of my writing with the addition of a single word or the suggestion of an alternate angle. The job of editing can be thankless. Let there be no mistake, Denise is deserving of my thanks.

This book never would have seen the light of day without the tireless efforts of my agent, Diana Flegal. Diana has believed in me from the start and never gave up on me. She is driven sheerly by her love of the Lord and her dedication to her authors, whom she shepherds with kindness.

Michael, my firstborn. I've never once heard you utter a harsh word. Your kindness and your belief in the dignity of all people are steadfast. You love people, animals, and fun. I'm immensely proud of you, and I love you more than I ever knew I could love anyone.

Stacey, my baby, my love. You bring more joy to my life than I could have ever imagined. You are constantly seeking ways to encourage and challenge people. You are warm and welcoming, always. Your sensitivity to the needs of others is uncanny. I treasure you.

Erikson, my newest son. God knew before He formed you that you would be Stacey's life partner. I could not have envisioned a more perfect husband for my daughter, or a more welcome addition to our family. I love you.

Steve, my husband, my life partner, my best friend. You were the love of my youth, the star of my young adulthood, the gem of my middle age and, God willing, you will be the pillar of my old age. I am yours and you are mine.

Table of Contents

≈

Foreword

It doesn't happen often.

I have read a lot of manuscripts over the years by aspiring writers, offering what help I can for the time I have. But I seldom see the result of their revisions. In this case, I did.

My response?

This woman has become a writer!

This woman is Sue Ciullo, and you will love her. You will love her honesty and her humility—from her stories about Lulu to strawberry wine to saying goodbye to her parents. The story about her mom will not only touch your heart but change your heart. Sue will walk you through the biblical stories, and, before you know it, you will be walking with her through her own stories and into yours. They will show you—rather than tell you—how to listen well, how to love well, how to serve well.

Most importantly, when you're finished with the book, you will discover—the way the two disciples did on the road to Emmaus—that it wasn't a stranger walking with you. It was Jesus.

~Ken Gire
Author of *Windows of the Soul*
and *Intimate Moments with the Savior*

Before You Begin

— ∾o∾ —

This book includes a retelling of stories from the Bible's New Testament. Although the thoughts and dialogue of the people involved have been invented, every effort has been made to respect the integrity of the biblical record.

Contemporary references throughout the book are factual. Some names have been changed to protect the privacy of the individuals portrayed.

Questions for personal reflection or group discussion are included after each chapter. If you're reading this book with a group, don't feel that you need to discuss all of the questions. Answer those questions that are meaningful to you. There are no right or wrong answers—simply contemplate the material presented and consider how it applies to your life.

The stories will benefit you most if you digest them slowly. They describe Jesus' interactions with ordinary men and women. Although these accounts describe brief encounters that occurred two thousand years ago, they have enormous practical application today. Meditate on their implications. Savor them. They shed light on the unique character of the carpenter from Galilee. No other person lived like He did, died like He did, or loved like He did.

I'm a mess, you're a mess, and we all need a Messiah.

I'm a mess.

It's true. Sometimes it's obvious. My actions, the scowl on my face, the tone of my voice—all reveal the turmoil of my soul.

Other times, it's not so apparent. I speak the right words and do the right things. I appear to have it all together. I'm courteous to strangers, leave generous tips for waiters, serve the poor with compassion, and demonstrate patience with my family and friends.

Sometimes I feel close to God. Other times, though, I've felt as far from God as dawn is from dusk. I wish I could say that I've figured out how to be good and that I won't mess up again. I know what it's like to walk in darkness, and I want no part of it any longer.

Confessing that I've messed up in the past isn't difficult. I've done terrible things, to be sure. I can reveal those things to people close to me. *It's okay,* I think. *They know I'm no longer like that. They know that now I try to do what's right.*

What's not so easy to confess is that I'm *still* a mess. My thoughts—those known only to me—regularly reveal my self-centeredness, judgmental attitude, haughtiness, and bitterness. Not quite so frequently, but still too often, my *actions* reveal what a mess I am. Walk into my office. Witness the stacks of unfiled papers, shirked responsibilities, unreturned phone calls, unpaid bills, and other uncompleted tasks. Follow me through my day and observe how I eat too much, spend too much, and care too little.

Other people probably don't like me much when I'm crabby, short-tempered, and irresponsible. They like me when I'm kind and compassionate. Nobody would love me if they saw only my contemptuous side, right? But my life, like yours, is a seesaw. Those who love me have seen not only the bad and the ugly in me but also the good. Surely, though, they love me because they first saw the good.

Somewhere in my upbringing, I was led to believe that God's love is like that—He loves me more when I speak the right words and do the right things. I was also told that God could read my thoughts—and that caused me shame. I wrongly assumed that if God knew my thoughts, He surely knew that I was a mess and, therefore, loved me less, if He loved me at all.

Still I wanted to learn something about this God whom, for my whole life, I had claimed to believe in. I had always identified myself as a Christian, but I didn't understand what that really meant. And who was this Jesus, anyway? I didn't just want to know *about* Him. I wanted to know Him.

The more I learned about Jesus, the more I wanted to learn about Him. The better I knew Jesus, the more I yearned to know

Him. I became enthralled and smitten. I was moved to shame for my sins and then refreshed by the forgiveness that, I eventually learned, was given freely to me. Gloriously, my eyes have been opened. I was blind, but now I see.

Through the years, what have I learned about this man called Jesus? Who was He? Who *is* He? Century after century, myriads of people from all nations have relied on Him for guidance, reassurance, peace, and love. And for eternal salvation.

Jesus walked the earth over two thousand years ago. Historians uniformly acknowledge His existence. He lived only thirty-three years. Most of what we know about His earthly life has been gleaned from the four gospels contained in the Bible's New Testament. These accounts were all written between thirty to sixty years following Jesus' brutal execution. Jesus' close friends, eyewitnesses to His remarkable life, wrote two of the accounts. The others were written by two of the earliest pioneers of the Christian movement, which began soon after Jesus' crucifixion and resurrection. Each gospel writer addressed a specific audience, and each had a specific purpose for recording the accounts.

Jesus was a teacher, a spiritual leader, and a miracle worker. The stories in this book, taken directly from the gospel accounts, reveal Jesus' nature and attributes. All that He did when He walked the earth was motivated by His love for people. As you read these pages, I pray that you'll feel the unconditional, unstoppable, incomprehensible love of this man we call Jesus.

Why is it important to get to know Jesus? Because I'm a mess, you're a mess, and we all need a Messiah.

But God demonstrates his own love for us in this:
While we were still sinners,
Christ died for us.
Romans 5:8

CHAPTER 1

Jesus Talks with the Woman at the Well

⌐∞⌐

Jesus knew the Pharisees had heard that he was baptizing and making more disciples than John (though Jesus himself didn't baptize them—-his disciples did). So he left Judea to return to Galilee. He had to go through Samaria on the way. Eventually he came to the Samaritan village of Sychar, near the field that Jacob gave to his son Joseph. Jacob's well was there; and Jesus, tired from the long walk, sat wearily beside the well about noontime.

Soon a Samaritan woman came to draw water, and Jesus said to her, "Please give me a drink." He was alone at the time because his disciples had gone into the village to buy some food.

The woman was surprised, for Jews refuse to have anything to do with Samaritans. She said to Jesus, "You are a Jew, and I am a Samaritan woman. Why are you asking me for a drink?"

Jesus replied, "If you only knew the gift God has for you and who you are speaking to, you would ask me, and I would give you living water."

"But sir, you don't have a rope or a bucket," she said, "and this well is very deep. Where would you get this living water? And besides, do you think you are greater than our ancestor Jacob, who gave us this well? How can you offer better water than he and his sons and his animals enjoyed?"

Jesus replied, "Anyone who drinks this water will soon become thirsty again. But those who drink the water I give will never be thirsty again. It becomes a fresh, bubbling spring within them, giving them eternal life."

"Please, sir," the woman said, "give me this water! Then I'll never be thirsty again, and I won't have to come here to get water."

"Go and get your husband," Jesus told her.

"I don't have a husband," the woman replied.

Jesus said, "You're right! You don't have a husband—for you have had five husbands, and you aren't even married to the man you're living with now."

"Sir," the woman said, "you must be a prophet. So tell me, why is it that you Jews insist that Jerusalem is the only place of worship, while we Samaritans claim it is here at Mount Gerizim, where our ancestors worshiped?"

Jesus replied, "Believe me, dear woman, the time is coming when it will no longer matter whether you worship the Father on this mountain or in Jerusalem. You Samaritans know very little about the one you worship, while we Jews know all about him, for salvation comes through the Jews. But the time is coming—indeed it's here now—when true worshipers will worship the Father in spirit and in truth. The Father is looking for those who will worship him that way. For God is Spirit, so those who worship him must worship in spirit and in truth."

The woman said, "I know the Messiah is coming—the one who is called the Christ. When he comes, he will explain everything to us."

Then Jesus told her, "I AM the Messiah!"

Just then his disciples came back. They were shocked to find him talking to a woman, but none of them had the nerve to ask, "What do you want with her?" or "Why are you talking to her?"

The woman left her water jar beside the well and ran back to the village, telling everyone, "Come and meet a man who told me *everything I ever did! Could he possibly be the Messiah?" So the people came streaming from the village to see him . . .*

Many Samaritans from the village believed in Jesus because the woman had said, "He told me everything I ever did!" When they came out to see him, they begged him to stay in their village. So he stayed for two days, long enough for many more to hear his message and believe. Then they said to the woman, "Now we believe, not just because of what you told us, but because we have heard him ourselves. Now we know that he is indeed the Savior of the world."

John 4:1-30, 39-42 (NLT)

Messiah to the Messed Up

She was a mess, this woman at the well. Unloved and unwanted. Rejected by all the respectable Jewish women. She was a failure. A first-century whore.

Why did Jesus approach the woman at the well? The encounter has intrigued people for the past two thousand years.

Jesus was a Jew. From childhood, He had studied the Jewish Bible. His family was devout. They observed the Jewish laws and customs. They carefully commemorated all the holidays—traditions ingrained in all devoted Jews.

Something else was also imbedded in the Jews: a hatred for the Samaritans. And the Samaritans reciprocated with intense loathing of the Jews. The mutual hatred sprouted from both religion and culture, firmly rooted for hundreds of years.[1]

The animosity began when Assyria conquered the northern kingdom of Israel in 722 BC. A large portion of the Jewish population was deported, and other peoples from the Assyrian Empire resettled in Israel. Jews and Gentiles, or non-Jewish colonists, then dwelt in the same territory and many intermarried. They were known as Samaritans and formed a sort of hybrid worship of God.

The Samaritans looked forward to the coming of the Messiah, as did the Jews. And although the Samaritans based their religion on the teachings of Moses, they did not adopt the rest of the Jewish Scriptures.

Intent on establishing a distinct religion, the Samaritans built their own temple on Mount Gerizim, claiming it as the holy place of worship. This was deplorable to the Jews, who claimed the sacred temple in Jerusalem was the true dwelling place of God. Finally, in 128 BC, the Jews destroyed the Samaritan temple. The Samaritans retaliated by littering the Jewish temple with human bones, rendering it defiled.[2]

Get the picture? This was no casual dislike. It was a mutual hatred that had been festering for over *seven hundred years*. From the time a child could speak he was taught, "They're no good. Stay away."

Jesus and His disciples were traveling from Judea to Galilee. By the time they reached the well near the town of Sychar in Samaria, they had been traveling by foot for about two days. Normally, devout Jews would add an additional day to their trip by avoiding Samaria altogether. But not Jesus. He chose the direct route, smack dab through Samaria.

When He arrived, Jesus was tired. He dripped with sweat and His mouth was parched. Two days of walking in sweltering heat on dirty, unpaved roads will do that to a man. Jesus took a seat, seeking rest by the well. Now, this wasn't just any well—it was *Jacob's Well*. That's right. The very well that had provided water to Jacob, grandson of Abraham, the mutual, beloved forefather of the Jews and the Samaritans.

After Jesus rested for a short while, He saw a woman approaching in the distance. Why was she coming to the well at midday, in the hot sun? Women normally came to draw water in the early morning or early evening when it was cooler—times when the women could mingle a bit and chitchat about neighborhood news and family events.

Maybe the other women ostracized her. Immorality was unacceptable. The town was small and everyone knew everyone. Did they view her as a threat to their own marriages? She certainly kept attracting men. After all, she had been married *five times*! Why did it always end badly? Did she keep picking losers? Maybe she kept finding her next catch while still married to her current husband.

We don't know why she had been married so many times, but we can surmise that she was a woman enveloped in deep pain. Her life was in shambles. Loneliness, insecurities, and shame held her captive.

This time around she hadn't even bothered with the formality of marriage—she was just shacking up with her current boyfriend. Not the kind of girl a guy would take home to meet his mother in first-century Palestine.

Why would Jesus, this popular rabbi approaching rock star status, approach *her*, of all people? Rabbis were forbidden from speaking with women in public, even their own mothers or sisters.

"Please give me a drink."

Imagine her surprise. *Now just who does he think he is? This Jew. Disgusting. Talking to me? A Samaritan. A woman.*

So she called Him on it. "Why are you asking me for a drink?" She expected a condescending response, but that isn't what she received.

"If you only knew the gift God has for you and who you are speaking to," Jesus said, "*you* would ask *me*, and I would give you living water." Such strange words. Intriguing words.

God has a gift—for me? And how could Jesus claim to have *living* water? Was He greater than their beloved ancestor, Jacob, who originally had the well dug?

But Jesus wasn't talking about water for her physical thirst. He was offering her something infinitely more valuable.

"Anyone who drinks this water will soon become thirsty again," Jesus told her. "But those who drink the water I give will never be thirsty again. It becomes a fresh, bubbling spring within them, giving them eternal life."

She still wasn't getting it. But she sensed something very different about this man. She actually bought into the idea of water that would quench her thirst *forever*! *I'm in,* she thought. *It's tough work hauling this water every day of my life.*

"Give me some of your living water, Jesus, so I can stop making this trek every single day."

Jesus knew that this woman's true thirst was of the spiritual variety, and He intended to offer her the only thing that could quench that thirst. But He needed her to shed the veil and fess up to her spiritual messed upness.

"Go and get your husband." With five words, Jesus exposed her.

"I don't have a husband," she admitted, her shame tumbling out, bared before His steady gaze.

"You're right! You don't have a husband—for you've had five husbands, and you aren't even married to the man you're living with now."

Whoa! How could this man possibly know these things? Clearly he is a holy prophet of God. He knows all about me. But how can this be? Despite all the sin, immorality, and shame that I bear, he spoke to me. He's kind to me—and I don't receive much kindness. I'm ashamed to be in his presence. To divert the focus from her faults, she changed the subject.

"Sir, you must be a prophet. Why is it that you Jews insist that Jerusalem is the only place of worship, while we Samaritans claim it is here at Mount Gerizim?"

Jesus let her know that the Jews had it right all along. They were worshiping God in the right place and way described in the Scriptures. But now that He had arrived, the issue of where to worship was moot.

"The time is coming—indeed it's here now," Jesus explained, "when true worshipers will worship the Father in Spirit and in truth."

Wow. This guy is deep. What does all this mean? I want to know more—so much more.

"I know the Messiah is coming—the one who is called the Christ. When He comes, He will explain everything to us."

Jesus' next statement rocked her world.

"I am the Messiah."

Can you imagine her reaction to that bombshell? The Jews and Samaritans had been waiting for the Messiah for hundreds of years. Now this guy comes and says *he's* the Messiah?

Just then the disciples returned. They saw Jesus talking with a woman and were dumbfounded. But hey, this was their rabbi, and they weren't about to call Him on it. The woman, though, figured it was time to hightail it out of there. She dropped her bucket and rushed to the village to tell everyone, "Come and see a man who told me everything I ever did! Could he possibly be the Messiah?"

So guess what? This woman of ill repute, *selected by Jesus*, became one of the first evangelists—and the very first *female* evangelist. No longer daunted by the chastisement she had faced, she boldly proclaimed the good news about the preacher from Nazareth. Many Samaritans believed in Jesus because of what the woman told them. They came to see Him and begged Him to stay. Jesus lingered with them for two days. Then many more believed because they heard Him themselves.

I never said hi to Lulu. She was a year younger than I was, and she had built up some notoriety with the guys in school. Word had it she was "easy." That made her kind of popular with some of the guys, if only behind closed doors, but we "nice girls"

snubbed her big time. When Lulu passed us in the halls, we murmured to one another, "There goes Lulu. Whore."

I had heard some rumblings that her home life was a little strange. She lived with her mother and some man who wasn't her dad. Maybe it was her mother's boyfriend; maybe it was an uncle. I never knew whether her dad had died or her parents were divorced.

None of that interested me. She was a whore as far as I was concerned, and that's all I needed to know. My friends felt the same way. How Lulu came to be promiscuous at such a young age was of no importance. Lulu became a factor in my life only when she decided to entertain my boyfriend and his friends one summer afternoon.

I had been going with him for about a year. At fifteen, I considered that a very long-term relationship, and I was crazy about him. I had been gradually realizing that he was not the guy for me, though. I still found him to be quite charming, but some problems were developing. He had begun to smoke pot, and he sometimes failed to call me when promised. I'd been contemplating breaking it off but hadn't yet been pushed that far. Then I heard about the incident with Lulu.

That's it, I concluded. And I ended my relationship with the guy.

During the years we attended the same school, there was never a time when I contemplated Lulu's well-being. I never invited her to go shopping or to hang out at McDonald's. She was a mess, and I wanted no part of her. My friends and I shunned her. I don't recall ever seeing her with another girl. The guys wouldn't be seen with her in public either. They did whatever it was they did in the privacy of someone's home while the parents were away. After they'd been properly served, she was dismissed.

Thinking about Lulu now, I get an ache in my gut. Lulu must have wakened each morning knowing that there would be no phone call from a friend, no greetings in the school halls, nobody to take an interest in her life. I wonder now whether the man who lived in her home had abused her. She probably wouldn't have offered her young body to any willing teenaged boy if someone, *anyone,* had told her that she counted for something, that she was better than that. I could have told her. But I didn't.

This man called Jesus. He captivates me for the same reasons He captivated the Samaritan woman at the well. Sure, He knew everything that she ever did. That's pretty amazing. But do you think that was what drew her in? I don't.

For me, it's personal. He broke through all of the barriers and social mores that destroy this messed up world. This rabbi was different. Not even a hint of misogyny. This teacher respected her as He would a man. Not a trace of bigotry either. This man valued her as He would a Jew. Not even the slightest iota of condescension. He gave her as much esteem as He would have given a close friend of high moral character. That's what grips me most. He looked straight past the sin and the shame in this messed up woman. And in Lulu. And in me. And in you. For me, it's His love.

We love because he first loved us.
1 John 4:19

Can You Relate?

Questions for Personal Reflection or Group Discussion

1. The Jews and the Samaritans had a fierce hatred of one another, based on both cultural and religious differences that had festered for hundreds of years.

    a. Describe a similar religious and cultural animosity that exists today.

    _____

    _____

    b. In the conflict that you described, which side do you think is "right"?

    _____

    _____

    c. Imagine you are stranded in a coffee shop during a fierce rainstorm. Only you and a person from the "wrong side" are in the coffee shop for the entire evening. How would you interact with this wayward stranger?

    _____

    _____

    d. If Jesus later made His way to the coffee shop, how do you think He would interact with the two of you?

    _____

    _____

2. What do you think motivated the woman at the well to rush to the village to tell everyone about Jesus?

_____

_____

3. Sue felt like she was better than Lulu, so Sue snubbed her.

  a. Think of someone that you've snubbed because you felt that you were better. If you could have a do-over, what would you do differently?

  _____

  _____

  b. Have you ever felt as if you were the Lulu, that is, not as good as the others in a group? If so, can you think of a kindness someone extended to you that touched your heart?

  _____

  _____

4. Which specific aspect of Jesus' meeting with the Samaritan woman at the well do you find particularly intriguing or touching?

_____

_____

5. As you reflect on their encounter, what strikes you about Jesus' character?

_____

_____

CHAPTER 2

Jesus Teaches the Disciples about Humility

People were bringing little children to Jesus for him to place his hands on them, but the disciples rebuked them. When Jesus saw this, he was indignant. He said to them, "Let the little children come to me, and do not hinder them, for the kingdom of God belongs to such as these. Truly I tell you, anyone who will not receive the kingdom of God like a little child will never enter it." And he took the children in his arms, put his hands on them and blessed them.

Mark 10:13-16

Advocate for the Humble

They were an unlikely group of friends. An eclectic bunch, to say the least. Jesus' disciples had little in common. They spanned a wide range of ages. They came from various towns of origin. Some were pragmatic and some were fiery. Four of them were fishermen. One was the lowest of the low, a tax collector. Most of them would not have chosen to be friends. But they had one critical thing in common: Jesus had chosen them.

Jesus was not your typical rabbi. No, He was a different kind of teacher. It seemed that nearly everything He did was unconventional. Young rabbis handpicked disciples to learn the "yoke"—the rabbi's interpretation of the Scriptures. Being selected as a disciple was a high honor. Most rabbis selected the crème de la crème as followers—those with exceptional intelligence, status, or reputation. Not Jesus. The disciples He selected had been passed over by other rabbis.

These twelve guys knew Jesus was up to something big. His reputation had begun to spread across the Judean countryside, so as Jesus invited each of them to follow Him, they knew He was inviting them to join a movement.

Jesus was about thirty years old when He began His public ministry. He met each disciple as He traveled throughout the Palestinian regions of Galilee and Judea. Jesus invited the men to follow Him. They became His apprentices and close friends. They traveled with Him, and while they did, He taught them a new way to live and began to transform their hearts. They needed to know these things so they could carry on His message after He was gone. Jesus knew what His disciples failed to grasp—that His walk on this earth would be brief. About three years later, He would be executed by crucifixion.

The disciples learned that Jesus had been raised in the region of Galilee in a town called Nazareth, a four-day walk from Jerusalem, which was the epicenter of Jewish society. The holy temple was there, and most Jews, including the disciples, made the trek to Jerusalem, by foot, to celebrate religious holidays.

Not only were Jesus' methods different from other rabbis, His demeanor was different too. He taught with an authority unmatched by anyone. His model was distinct. Exciting. Crowds of people took note of Jesus' teachings as He spoke in the synagogues, in the courts of the holy temple, and before large crowds on the mountainsides of Galilee.

Jesus preached a new message. He emphasized a new way to live, a way to be transformed from the inside out. He taught that many who were viewed as powerful and mighty in this world were the least in God's eyes. He explained that God wasn't pleased by an outward compliance to rules and regulations; rather, God wanted the people's hearts to be transformed. He wanted them to love God and to love one another. Jesus' words penetrated the souls of His listeners:

Blessed are the poor in spirit, for theirs is the kingdom of heaven.

Blessed are those who mourn, for they will be comforted.

Blessed are the meek, for they will inherit the earth.

Blessed are the pure in heart, for they will see God.

Blessed are those who are persecuted because of righteousness, for theirs is the kingdom of heaven.[3]

15

The kingdom of heaven and the kingdom of God were terms Jesus used often. The phrases refer to the reign of God. And in God's kingdom, His subjects would reap His benevolence. Jesus told His disciples the kingdom of heaven was near, or the kingdom of God was at hand. His words excited the Jews, who had been under Roman rule for the past one hundred years.

In fact, God's kingdom *was* at hand. Jesus *had* come to deliver them. But not in the way they expected. They expected their Messiah to be a sort of military leader who would launch a revolt, throw the Roman occupation force out of the land, and establish Jewish supremacy. The Jews were expecting a warrior, which Jesus was. They just weren't expecting a warrior with gentle hands.[4] No, the disciples didn't yet understand the methods God was using to establish the kingdom of heaven. But they understood it was near. That truth was electrifying!

Jesus delivered thrilling teachings, indeed, but He also delivered amazing healings. Throughout the countryside, Jesus moved from town to town, healing those who were afflicted with disease.

First-century Palestine was not a compassionate society. Those with diseases were summarily cast out from society. Most people believed that if someone had a birth defect or illness, they or their parents had done something sinful to summon God's punishment. If they were blind or had physical disabilities, no social services were available—no Salvation Army, no March of Dimes, no Medicaid. They became homeless beggars, loitering near the gates of the synagogue, hoping to receive enough alms to stay alive. If people had a skin disease, they were considered unclean—forbidden from touching *anyone* and banished from the synagogue.

To be put out of the synagogue was no small deal. Each town had a synagogue, where everyone gathered on the Sabbath for worship and to study Scripture. During the week, the synagogue served as the community center, the government center, and the school. The leaders of the synagogue were the municipal authorities of the community. So to be put out of the synagogue didn't just mean you couldn't attend the weekly worship service—it meant you were simply *no good*.

Just imagine. Into this mess walks Jesus. Oozing love. Radiating compassion. Validating the worth of every individual. Giving people hope. Healing their bodies. Comforting their souls.

Throngs of people followed this preacher throughout Palestine. To have solitude or time to pray, Jesus arose very early in the morning and retreated to an isolated place. Scripture tells us that on at least one occasion he had to "withdraw by boat, privately to a solitary place,"[5] and the crowds *still* followed Him by foot to the town at the other side of the lake. There were no paparazzi, but Jesus was drawing huge crowds of the Elvis variety, two thousand years before Elvis lived.

Into this setting arrived the children. Parents came, bringing their young ones, so Jesus could bless them.

Can you imagine what the disciples were thinking as the parents pushed their children toward Jesus? *Oh, isn't this just great? The Master can barely get a moment to Himself and here come these parents with their little kids. Don't they know He has more important things to do than to spend His time touching children? There are people to cure, sermons to preach. "Bless my children." Oh, come on already. Jesus doesn't have time for such unimportant things.*

But the disciples should have known better. Hadn't they been traveling with Jesus? Hadn't they heard Him address the people? Had they totally missed the message that the masses were devouring? "Blessed are the pure in heart, for they will see

17

God. Blessed are the meek," Jesus had said, "for they will inherit the earth."

I ask you, who is meeker than a little child? No wonder Jesus was indignant. Jesus had been teaching a new message of mercy, and the disciples were working as bouncers. Jesus knew that they would be teaching His message after He was gone and that the time of His departure was not far away. He seized every opportunity to teach them. "Let the little children come to me, and do not hinder them, for the kingdom of God belongs to such as these. Truly I tell you, anyone who will not receive the kingdom of God like a little child will never enter it."

In another encounter, some of Jesus' disciples asked Him who would be considered the greatest in the kingdom of heaven. These guys, traveling companions of the famous Jesus, thought they were pretty hot stuff. Surely they would rank high in that kingdom. Then Jesus called a little boy and placed him in the middle of the group: "Unless you change and become like little children, you will never enter the kingdom of heaven. Therefore, whoever takes the lowly position of this child is the greatest in the kingdom of heaven."[6]

The disciples thought that they had it all locked up. In the kingdom of heaven, they would be considered great. No, Jesus said. In fact, unless they had a major attitude adjustment, they wouldn't even get past the gatekeepers of heaven.

To enter the kingdom of heaven, we must realize that we cannot earn that privilege. We can only enter by the grace of Jesus, our benevolent host. Neither our actions nor our imagined greatness can buy us an entry ticket. Jesus paid that price on the cross. The invitation is open to all. But only those who humble themselves and accept His mercy will be admitted.

Kirsten and Scott Strand are examples of pure humility. Their lives illustrate the type of meekness Jesus advocated. From the start, their marriage has been centered on discovering God's will for their lives and living it out. Their family's mission is this: *We will grow in our understanding of human suffering and how we are called to make a difference.* Each year they hold a family summit at a secluded cabin. During their family weekend, they put together a focus for the year ahead, seeking to discover what God is calling them to do. They describe themselves as a missional family. And missional they are.

The year 2003 was pivotal for the Strands. Scott had a lucrative career as a regional account manager in the biochemistry field. Kirsten was a stay-at-home mom, taking care of their two young sons. She also worked part time in ministry at her church, serving the poor. They lived in a lovely, upscale home in a fashionable neighborhood. But their hearts were unsettled.

Scott had long desired to be a teacher. But since he was in his thirties and well established in a profitable career, it seemed impractical. However, God convinced them that if they were to be true to their mission, they couldn't let "little things" like money, status, comfort, or fear keep them from making the most of the one life they had been given.

So one day, Scott walked into his boss's office and submitted his resignation. He went from being a major breadwinner to being Mr. Mom by day and college student by night.

That same year, Kirsten devoted her life to helping her church find ways to show the love of Jesus to the marginalized in their midst. She became the director of a ministry called Community 4:12, devoted to serving the poor. Under Kirsten's leadership,

Community 4:12 began a concerted effort to enhance the lives of the people in an impoverished area of a nearby city, East Aurora. The organization works through the public schools to enrich the lives of the students and their families.

Three years later, Scott started a new job as a third grade teacher. He could have worked in almost any school district. But Scott wanted to make an impact on the lives of the students and families he and Kirsten had been serving. So "Mr. Strand" became the newest member of the faculty at Bardwell Elementary School in East Aurora, IL.

In the years since Kirsten took on the role of Director of Community 4:12, she has mobilized thousands of people both to form relationships with the poor and to become involved in improving their lives.

Each week, volunteers mentor and tutor students. Each autumn, Community 4:12 hosts a back-to-school sponsorship program in which those who are financially blessed sponsor kids so they can head off to school with a new backpack loaded with essential supplies. Each winter there is a huge Christmas Gift Mart where parents of school kids can buy gifts for their children at greatly reduced prices, made possible by the thousands of gifts contributed by members of local churches and patrons of neighboring businesses. Merchants from nearby communities contribute their time and supplies to serve the families coffee and hot chocolate on the cold winter morning of the Gift Mart. The smiles on the faces of parents who have purchased gifts for their kids to open on Christmas Eve are priceless. They know that without this outpouring of Christian kindness, there might have been no gifts at all.

Community 4:12 serves the disadvantaged in the city in many other ways too. The lives of those in the community have been changed dramatically. The lives of the thousands who serve have been radically enriched as well. All this happened because Kirsten and Scott Strand rose up to do what God called them to do.

Something else is noteworthy about the Strands. The year after Scott began teaching, they decided to sell their beautiful home in their upscale community and move to the inner city neighborhood they served.

"Jesus relocated," explained Kirsten. "He became one of us. He didn't commute back and forth to heaven. Similarly, the best way for us to love the poor is to become their neighbors. If I am living in a poor community, then I suddenly have a much more personal interest in making sure schools provide quality education, the streets are safe to walk, and the houses on my street are not dilapidated. Suddenly, poverty is not something that affects 'them'—it affects 'me'."

Spurred on with that divine insight, they traded in their lifestyle of the privileged to take on the lifestyle of the underprivileged and moved to the community they serve.

Yes, the Strands are truly inspirational, and I am blessed to call them friends. If anyone has the right to boast of their good works, Kirsten and Scott do. But here's the thing: they are truly the most humble couple I've ever known. The local media is always interested in Community 4:12 events. Newspapers cover the festivities and lots of photos are taken. Kirsten and Scott are rarely photographed, though. They prefer to be in the background. Try to commend them for their amazing works, and they will point instead to the thousands of volunteers who commit their time and resources to serve the community. Tell them that they are the driving force, and they will tell you that they are the most dispensable people on the team. And they mean it.

So what did Jesus mean when He told the disciples to receive the kingdom of God like little children? The disciples already knew the answer. Jesus' teaching had been clear. God's kingdom belongs to the poor in spirit, the excluded, the suffering—not the proud, mighty, and self-sufficient. All of that was reflected in the message He taught the crowds.

Bring the children to me, Jesus said. To enter the kingdom of God, everyone needs to become like children. They need to descend from their self-built pedestals and become truly humble.

Kirsten and Scott Strand learned that lesson. They learned that their worth wasn't found in high-paying careers, an upscale home, and high-end cars. They laid these things aside, eager to spend their time doing the work God laid before them. They learned true humility and, in doing so, have devoted their lives to serving those most in need. This is the love that Jesus demonstrated. This was His message.

It took the disciples a while to learn, but they did become like children. They also learned the lesson of humility. So great was the love of the preacher from Nazareth, that they gave away everything they previously had struggled to achieve. They were overwhelmed by the love of their friend and compelled to love others in gratitude to Jesus. They had been called to make a difference, and they carried out that mission. They changed the trajectory of their lives. In doing so, they changed the trajectory of the world. Gone were the days of bickering over who would be considered great. These men had absolute heart knowledge of this truth: their value came directly from the God they served.

Do nothing out of selfish ambition or vain conceit. Rather, in humility value others above yourselves.
Philippians 2:3

Can You Relate?

Questions for Personal Reflection or Group Discussion

1. The disciples were Jesus' constant traveling companions. More than anyone else, they should have understood His message. What do you think kept them from understanding the message Jesus consistently spoke and lived out?

   _____

   _____

2. Upon reflection, do you think you are sometimes resistant to the message Jesus consistently spoke and lived out? If so, what do you think is the cause of that resistance?

   _____

   _____

3. The disciples thought they could earn a place of honor in Jesus' kingdom because they were His close friends and they were doing good things. Have you ever thought that entry into heaven is an honor that can be earned by going to church and doing good things?

   _____

   _____

4. Jesus said, "Blessed are the meek, for they shall inherit the earth." What do you think He meant by that?

   _____

   _____

5. Kirsten and Scott Strand are living out humility by rising up to serve the poor as God called them to do. They are transforming a community and transforming hearts. Think of someone who has sacrificed their own comfort to do the work God has called them to do.

    a. What impact has that person had on others?

    _____

    _____

    b. Do you think it was difficult for that individual to do the work they felt called to do?

    _____

    _____

    c. How has their decision affected their own life and the lives of those they love?

    _____

    _____

    d. Share, if you choose, something you feel God is calling you to do.

    _____

    _____

    e. What reservations do you have about doing it?

    _____

    _____

    f. Today, consider asking God how you may be obedient to what He has laid on your heart.

    _____

    _____

CHAPTER 3

Jesus Challenges the Rich Young Man

As Jesus started on his way, a man ran up to him and fell on his knees before him. "Good teacher," he asked, "what must I do to inherit eternal life?"

"Why do you call me good?" Jesus answered. "No one is good—except God alone. You know the commandments: 'You shall not murder, you shall not commit adultery, you shall not steal, you shall not give false testimony, you shall not defraud, honor your father and mother'."

"Teacher," he declared, "all these I have kept since I was a boy."

Jesus looked at him and loved him. "One thing you lack," he said. "Go, sell everything you have and give to the poor, and you will have treasure in heaven. Then come, follow me."

At this the man's face fell. He went away sad, because he had great wealth.

Jesus looked around and said to his disciples, "How hard it is for the rich to enter the kingdom of God!"

The disciples were amazed at his words. But Jesus said again, "Children, how hard it is to enter the kingdom of God! It is easier for a camel to go through the eye of a needle than for someone who is rich to enter the kingdom of God."

The disciples were even more amazed, and said to each other, "Who then can be saved?"

Jesus looked at them and said, "With man this is impossible, but not with God; all things are possible with God."

Then Peter spoke up, "We have left everything to follow you!"

"Truly I tell you," Jesus replied, "no one who has left home or brothers or sisters or mother or father or children or fields for me and the gospel will fail to receive a hundred times as much in this present age: homes, brothers, sisters, mothers, children and fields—along with persecutions—and in the age to come eternal life. But many who are first will be last, and the last first."

Mark 10:17-31

Lover of Lost Souls

So close, yet so far. The rich young man who approached Jesus had a lot going for him. He was wealthy and powerful but also kind-hearted. He treated people well. Yet, in spite of his stellar qualities, he knew in his heart that he fell short. He understood that there was a life beyond this earthly life, and he wanted an entry ticket.

He had heard of Jesus, the traveling preacher. Indeed, who hadn't? He knew about the throngs of people this merciful Jesus had healed through God's power. This man did not seek Jesus out for healing, though. He sensed so much more in this rabbi. When he approached Jesus, he did it openly. He set aside the haughtiness of his high position and knelt before Jesus. He used a term not used by his Jewish contemporaries. "Good teacher," he called Jesus. And that term, "good," was reserved at the time only for the one true God.[7] Yes, this guy was on to something. *The renowned Jesus of Nazareth. He is no ordinary preacher,* he thought. *Only through God's power can he heal. And he speaks with authority that can only come from the one true God.*

So this young man extended to Jesus a humble demonstration of that insight. When he saw Jesus, he fell on his knees before Him and acknowledged Him as an affiliate of God. "Good teacher. I know I've got it all now. But I want more. I want eternal life. And I know I haven't earned it. What do I need to do?"

Jesus gave this guy the credit that was due to him for

recognizing divinity in his midst. "Why do you call me good? No one is good—except God alone."

Jesus immediately recognized an error in this man's theology, though. This fellow thought he could gain eternal life by doing good things—a common belief—then and now. So Jesus recited commandments to him. Not all ten commandments. The first four commandments focus on loving God. The last six emphasize loving people—those are the ones Jesus recited to him. The man thought he had done a good job with those commandments, and that was probably true. Not perfect, but pretty good.

But pretty good is not enough to earn everlasting life. How could any mere man possibly *earn* his way to living eternally with an all-holy God? Fortunately, the all-loving Father had that plan all worked out. And that plan centered on Jesus, His Son.

Jesus realized the young ruler lacked heartfelt devotion to God. Instead, he was devoted to his wealth and all its perks. Jesus wanted so much more for him. He looked right past his fine clothing and polished exterior, straight through to his soul, a soul clinging to the things he could never bring with him to the eternal life that he came seeking. One day, all those things would turn to dust.

"One thing you lack," Jesus told him. This man's temporary wealth paled in comparison to the riches Jesus offered. "Go, sell everything you have and give to the poor, and you will have treasure in heaven. Then come, follow me."

Think about what Jesus was offering. A chance to follow *Him*, the Messiah promised by God. Prophets had foretold His coming for centuries. Generation after generation sought Him—and here He was. The young man stood nose to nose with the Messiah. But this man was too wrapped up in his stuff. He wanted to gain eternal life, sure, but give away all his stuff to the poor? *Jesus, I wanted an easy answer. Couldn't You just tell me something I could do with my excess?* To give up comfort, security, and power was just too much to ask. *Can't do it, Jesus. I* am *my stuff.* This man had a great big affluence problem. His wealth, not God, was the true stronghold of his heart. So given the chance to follow God's own Son, he took a pass.

Jesus had offered others the same chance to follow Him. He chose twelve disciples to befriend and train during His three-year ministry. These men (minus the infamous Judas) went on after Jesus' ascension to establish the Christian church, which remains the stalwart of civilization to this day.

Scripture tells us that in addition to the twelve, Jesus was looking for seventy-two men to precede Him and His disciples to towns that they intended to visit.[8] Their mission was to heal the sick in the name of God and to announce the coming of the Messiah. Surely, every one of them had things going on in their lives that could have held them back. But these followers accepted the invitation eagerly, giving up the comfort of their homes and their jobs, and the nearness of their families and worldly goods. They took a pass on any goodbye feasts and decided to follow Jesus. And they were instrumental in changing the course of the world.

Scripture is rich with examples of Jesus inviting people to follow Him. When Jesus extended the invitation to one such man, he replied, "Lord, first let me go and bury my father."[9] That doesn't mean the man's father was dead. In first-century Palestine, immediately upon the death of a parent, the eldest son closed the eyes of his mother or father. A drumbeat announced the death, and all work in the village stopped. Rituals were of great importance as are funeral rituals of any culture today. If the man's father had been deceased, he would have been buried the same day; therefore, the man certainly could have met up with Jesus the following day. No, this guy had an elderly father, and he didn't want to follow Jesus until his father had died. How did Jesus respond? "Let the dead bury their own dead. But you go and proclaim the kingdom of God."

Another man told Jesus, "I will follow you, Lord; but first let me go back and say goodbye to my family."[10] And Jesus told him, "No one who puts his hand to the plow and looks back is fit for service in the kingdom of God." Does that sound harsh? Maybe, but here's the point: in each case, Jesus saw the heart condition of these men. No, it's not loyalty to father or family that Jesus admonishes. It's lack of devotion to Him. Jesus knows what impediments keep us from following Him, even when we ourselves deny them.

The rich young man was wealthy in material things alone. Those things would wither.

Like the guy in the story, maybe you're a person who has a lot of money. Maybe you hang your head low when reading this story. Or maybe your material goods are meager by comparison. Does this story condemn the wealthy? Does it give a Get-into-Heaven-Free Card for those who have less? Actually, this story neither condemns the rich nor fast-tracks the poor. This is a story about devotion, about the condition of the heart. And the heart of the man in our story was devoted to his money.

Contrast his story with that of Melissa and Fred. Fred is the breadwinner in the family. He's been blessed with a sharp intellect, keen business savvy, passion, and drive. His wife,

Melissa, while receiving no monetary income, works harder than most anyone I know. She is a Bible study facilitator and administrator; event planner; women, youth and young adult advocate and encourager; and a church elder. Her faith is strong and her heart is pure. Melissa sees, really *sees*, lost or hurting people whom most everyone else overlooks. She recognizes them, seeks them out, lifts them up, and loves them.

Melissa and Fred have servant hearts. They have humbly served on mission trips abroad. They have a fervent love and compassion for impoverished, sick, orphaned, and widowed people in Africa. Fred serves on the board of directors of Global Family Rescue, a nonprofit, faith-based charitable organization passionately dedicated to bringing hope to families living in extreme poverty throughout the world.

Fred and Melissa have hearts that naturally befriend the poor. To say they *serve* the poor would be inaccurate. Instead, they form relationships with the financially unfortunate. They do not see the poor as "service projects." They see them as friends.

Fred and Melissa regularly perform impassioned acts of kindness for those in need, for their neighbors near and far. They have two young adult sons. Both are tenderhearted like their parents.

The income Fred earns as a marketing executive has enabled his family to move into a spacious, stunning home in an upscale community. Like the man in our story, Melissa and Fred have great wealth. But their wealth does not possess them. On the contrary, they are extremely generous. They use their wealth to serve others. They often welcome guests into their home for days, weeks, or months. They have repeatedly opened their home to friends or acquaintances down on their luck. They receive guests warmly and offer them a comfortable place to live while they work out their circumstances.

I know Fred and Melissa well and can testify that their wealth is not the focus of their lives. It certainly does not define them. The focus of their lives is Jesus. Fred and Melissa are centered on Him. They have a passion for Jesus Christ. Their true wealth lies in their devotion to Him.

My life often resembles those who took a pass on following Jesus. I let life get in the way of my passion for Him. I tell myself that I'll read more Scripture, contribute my talents to those in need, minister to the poor, visit the elderly, and comfort the bereaved when my life settles down. The reasons for my disengagement vary with the season of my life: When my kids are older. When my workload becomes more manageable. When my parents have passed on. When I'm not so tired. When I'm healthier. When I retire. And each reason seems valid at the time. But when I honestly examine my motives, I'm convicted with the truth that each of these deterrents reflects the state of my soul. Each instance reveals that God has been second in my life, or maybe third, or fourth.

In fact, Jesus extends the invitation to follow Him to each of us. I'm convinced that even those who have never read a single Bible passage feel the tugging of God on their heartstrings. In *Confessions* Saint Augustine said, "You have created us for yourself, O Lord, and our hearts are restless until they rest in you."[11] There is a God-shaped hole in our hearts and the void can be filled by no other means. Not by wealth, power, sex, drugs, accomplishments, or relationships. The God-shaped hole can only be filled by choosing to follow the Creator who loves you. That's the bottom line: the all-powerful Creator sent His only Son to lead us to Him *because He loves us.*

I'm drawn to the story of the rich young man again and again. Yes, he went away sad because he had great wealth. But above all else, one thing tugs at the strings of my heart when I read about Jesus' encounter with this wealthy man: "Jesus looked at him and loved him."

But you, Lord, are a compassionate and gracious God, slow to
anger, abounding in love and faithfulness.
Psalm 86:15

Can You Relate?

Questions for Personal Reflection or Group Discussion

1. Do you think the rich young man felt differently about his wealth after meeting Jesus? Why or why not?

   _____

   _____

2. Think of someone you know who is wealthy, but whom you pity. What appears to be the focus of this person's life?

   _____

   _____

3. Think of someone you know who is wealthy and whom you admire. What appears to be the focus of this person's life?

   _____

   _____

4. Describe someone you know who has meager material things, but whom you admire. What is it you admire about this person?

   _____

   _____

5. Looking back on your own life, do you think you have been happiest when you have been most prosperous? Why or why not?

   _____

   _____

6. Jesus said that it is easier for a camel to go through the eye of a needle than for a rich man to enter the kingdom of God, but that with God all things are possible. He is pointing out that it is much harder for the rich to enter heaven than for those who are poor. Why do you think it is harder for the rich to enter heaven?

   _____

   _____

7. Can you think of any people from the Bible who were wealthy and also part of "God's kingdom?" If so, who? Why were they allowed to enter God's kingdom?

   _____

   _____

8. What other things can make it hard for a person to enter God's kingdom?

   _____

   _____

9. Share, if you choose, some things that make it hard for you to follow Jesus. In what ways are you similar to the rich young man who came to see Jesus?

   _____

   _____

CHAPTER 4

Jesus Protects the Adulterous Woman

At dawn he appeared again in the temple courts, where all the people gathered around him, and he sat down to teach them. The teachers of the law and the Pharisees brought in a woman caught in adultery. They made her stand before the group and said to Jesus, "Teacher, this woman was caught in the act of adultery. In the Law Moses commanded us to stone such women. Now what do you say?" They were using this question as a trap, in order to have a basis for accusing him.

But Jesus bent down and started to write on the ground with his finger. When they kept on questioning him, he straightened up and said to them, "Let any one of you who is without sin be the first to throw a stone at her." Again he stooped down and wrote on the ground.

At this, those who heard began to go away one at a time, the older ones first, until only Jesus was left, with the woman still standing there. Jesus straightened up and asked her, "Woman, where

37

are they? Has no one condemned you?"

"No one, sir," she said.

"Then neither do I condemn you," Jesus declared. "Go now and leave your life of sin."

John 8:2-11

Merciful Master

The woman standing in the temple court was in a heap of trouble. She'd been caught in the very act of committing adultery. Adultery is a serious offense today, but in first-century Palestine, there were additional nuances to consider.

The definition of adultery was very specific. Sexual relations between a married or betrothed woman and any man other than her husband were adulterous acts. Adultery, therefore, was committed only against a husband, never against a wife.[12] Adultery was regarded as a great social wrong and a serious sin on the part of both the man and woman participating in the sexual act. Mosaic Law dictated that both the adulterer and the adulteress were to be executed. The accuser was to cast the first stone or rock, with the community members continuing to hurl stones until the guilty parties died. The Bible doesn't record any instances of this punishment actually being carried out for the crime of adultery; nevertheless, the prescribed legal penalty for the perpetrators was death.

The religious leaders in Jerusalem, who considered Jesus a serious threat to the status quo, had been trying to find a valid reason to have Him arrested and put to death. In this particular attempt, they brought a woman who had been caught in the act of adultery before a crowd gathered in the temple courts. To catch her in the act would be pretty difficult, right? And if she *had* indeed been caught in the act, where was her co-defendant, her sexual partner? The entire scenario seems suspicious—as if this woman had been set up in order to, in turn, set up Jesus. One thing is clear: the religious leaders weren't motivated by any desire to uphold the teachings of the Law. Neither were they interested in carrying out justice. If those had been their objectives, certainly the woman's partner would have been brought before Jesus with her.

Therefore, the conniving religious leaders, in this instance the teachers of the Law and the Pharisees, brought the accused woman before Jesus to trap Him. "Teacher, this woman was caught in the act of adultery. In the Law, Moses commanded us to stone such a woman. Now what do you say?"

They believed they had given Him a no-win situation. They assumed Jesus had only two choices: yes or no.

If He said yes, the Roman authorities would likely indict Him, since only the Roman government held the legal right to issue the death penalty. Even without such an indictment, Jesus would lose His status as the merciful master, the forgiver of sins. He could no longer retain the position of preeminent leader of the masses. Instead, He would be known as the one who led this woman to her death.

On the other hand, if He said, "No, don't stone her," He would be publicly violating their sacred law. They had presented Jesus with a lose-lose situation and anticipated their victory, which they believed was close at hand.

What a stunning scene it must have been. The woman standing before them, her nudity having been hastily concealed by a simple frock before her accusers dragged her before the crowd. Shivering with fear, she was surely feeling that, in addition to her utter shame, she was about to be executed.

The crowd was composed of Jesus' followers. They had come to hear Him teach in the temple courts. They had been drawn by

His message of love and compassion. Would they now be made to participate in a brutal act of execution? Would they ever be able to wash her death, by their own hands, from their souls? Would they forever see her mutilated body when they closed their eyes to sleep?

The pretentious religious leaders stood ready, waiting for the trap to snap and finally snare this nuisance of a preacher. At last, they would have the evidence they needed to convict Him, send Him to His death, and be rid of Him forever.

Every eye was on Jesus. Every ear fervently listened for His response. And what did Jesus do? He stooped down, wrote on the ground in the temple courtyard, and continued with His lesson. The religious leaders hadn't anticipated that! And they could not let Him escape the consequences that His answer to their question would bring.

So they pressed Him. "What do you say, Jesus?"

Jesus straightened and answered, "Let any one of you who is without sin be the first to throw a stone at her."

Imagine the various reactions of those witnessing this scene. The woman, still in fear, but praying for dispensation and hoping beyond hope, *Could my life possibly be spared?*

Jesus' followers must have been thankful they wouldn't be forced to participate in the woman's execution. Perhaps some in the crowd had committed the same sin. Most others had certainly perpetrated the same transgression in their heart at some time during their lives—lusting after someone to whom they were not married.

And the religious leaders? Could they claim to be sinless? Or did they know that the fate of this woman might truly be their own if the many stipulations of the Law were enforced?

So the crowd dispersed, the accusers and the students of

Jesus' teachings alike. The old left first, their heads hung low. They were the elders, who were esteemed by the younger people present, but who had amassed a vast list of sins during their lives. The young soon followed, each with their respective inventory of sins and shame buried in their hearts.

Each person knew the woman's fate might well have been his own. Each knew that in Jesus' merciful, masterful sparing of this woman, He also made mercy available to them. They didn't know what price Jesus would pay to render that mercy. His death by crucifixion as the final perfect price for all sins was yet to be paid. But everyone understood the dramatic mercy He rendered that morning in the temple courts.

I too have received mercy on many occasions. One such instance took place when I was a teenager. At about the age of fifteen, I went out one cool May Friday evening with some friends. As was our ritual at the time, my friends and I scored some cheap wine by standing outside the local liquor store and imploring an approaching customer to take our money and add a couple of bottles of Boone's Farm Strawberry Hill to his order. Ten minutes later we left, wine in hand, and headed to a night of raucous fun. On that particular night, we gathered at the home of a friend whose parents were out of town for the weekend. Always one to dive right in, I drank far more than I could handle and became very drunk, very quickly.

But the night was still young. At some point during the evening, we dispersed into several smaller groups. Some of us left the party, moving our merriment to the streets. We shared a myriad of laughs. Everything seemed far funnier than it truly was. We roared boisterously on those suburban streets.

Some passing police officers noticed our antics and tracked down one of my friends, Kathy. When they found her, she actually had tire tracks on her face from lying against a car in her drunken stupor. That memory still sends my friends and me into fits of laughter decades later. The police failed to recognize the hilarity of the scene, though. They picked Kathy up and delivered her home to her mother, who was, of course, mortified to see her daughter in such a condition.

After tending to her daughter, Kathy's mother called mine to ask if I had shared in the shenanigans. The call came shortly after I had returned home. I had told my mom that I'd spent a mellow evening with my friends and that I was going to bed.

"Marian, this is Rose. Is Mary Sue home?"

"Yeah, but she just went up to bed. Why do you ask?"

"Well, some cops just deposited Kathy on my front porch. She's stinkin' drunk. I know she was out with Mary Sue, so I figure she must be wasted too."

"Oh, I'm sorry to hear that, Rose, but Sue doesn't drink. She talked with me before heading up to bed and she's fine, really. Thanks for the call, though. I hope Kathy will sleep it off and wake up feeling much better."

But just to be sure, Mom came to my room to check on me. I was *not* fine. To her dismay, she found me sleeping in my own vomit, nearly unconscious, too sick to lift my head. Her maternal love spurred her into immediate action. She lifted me from my bed and led me to the bathroom. Once there she removed my vile pajamas, saturated with puke. She drew a warm bath for me and told me to get in. Then she washed my hair and gave me a soapy washcloth so I could clean my body. When I

43

was finished, she helped me out of the bathtub, then gave me a towel and some clean pajamas. After I put them on, she led me back to bed. While I was in the bathroom, she had removed the putrid linens and replaced them with fresh ones.

That was almost forty years ago, and as I recall the incident, I'm still drenched with shame. I had betrayed my mom by drinking the wine and by getting obscenely drunk. And there was the shame of my nakedness. At fifteen, I was far past the age where it was acceptable for my mother to see me naked. But I had left her no choice. She was compelled to care for me, and that included helping me bathe.

During the entire ordeal, she didn't yell at me. She didn't chastise or lecture me. I figured that would come the next day, when I could take it all in. But the next day came and there was no lecture, no rebuke, and no punishment. I was neither grounded nor derided. Mom didn't tell me how disappointed she was in me, but I knew I had betrayed her trust. The dreaded punishment never came, and that is the point of this story.

The next Friday night came, along with the usual invitation to buy a bottle of Boone's Farm Strawberry Hill and to head out for another night of fun with friends. I declined. "My mother is the definition of grace," I said. "I cannot let her down."

I can relate to the woman brought before Jesus. Her sin was exposed before the crowd at the temple and before the teacher named Jesus. How ashamed she must have been. How she dreaded her punishment, which would be delivered swiftly. But the punishment never came. Jesus intervened on her behalf. He did not excuse her sin as it was quite serious. Instead He showed mercy. As He always did, He saw straight through to her heart. He saw her shame and her remorse after her sin was exposed. He knew how His compassion had affected her. Jesus told her that He did not condemn her, but that she should leave her life of sin. Surely her heart, entirely grateful and teachable, convicted her and prompted her to abandon her sinful lifestyle. Jesus' tenderness had pierced her soul. She had met the embodiment of grace, love, mercy, and compassion. How could she betray the mercy of her Savior or reject His love?

Because of God's tender mercy,
the morning light from heaven
is about to break upon us.
Luke 1:78 (NLT)

Can You Relate?

1. When have you felt compelled to judge others' actions? What factors caused you to desire punishment for those actions?

    _____

    _____

2. When have you felt compelled to forgive without punishing others' actions? What factors caused you to bestow mercy?

    _____

    _____

3. Think of a time when someone showed you mercy—forgiving something you had done without seeking to punish you. How did their act of mercy affect you?

    _____

    _____

4. Jesus acknowledged that the woman brought before Him was an adulteress. Why do you think He chose to save her?

    _____

    _____

5. Considering Jesus' reaction to the adulterous woman, how do you think He feels about you and your sins?

    _____

    _____

6. As you reflect on Jesus' interaction with the adulterous woman, which of His character traits stand out?

_____

_____

7. How does Jesus' mercy to the adulterous woman make you feel about Him?

_____

_____

CHAPTER 5

Jesus Dines with Zacchaeus

Jesus entered Jericho and was passing through. A man was there by the name of Zacchaeus; he was a chief tax collector and was wealthy. He wanted to see who Jesus was, but because he was short he could not see over the crowd. So he ran ahead and climbed a sycamore-fig tree to see him, since Jesus was coming that way.

When Jesus reached the spot, he looked up and said to him, "Zacchaeus, come down immediately. I must stay at your house today." So he came down at once and welcomed him gladly.

All the people saw this and began to mutter, "He has gone to be the guest of a sinner."

But Zacchaeus stood up and said to the Lord, "Look, Lord! Here and now I give half of my possessions to the poor, and if I have cheated anybody out of anything, I will pay back four times the amount."

Jesus said to him, "Today salvation has come to this house, because this man, too, is a son of Abraham. For the Son of Man came to seek and to save the lost."

Luke 19:1-10

Friend of Sinners

Zacchaeus had arrived. He'd hit the big time. He was on top of the world.

Zacchaeus was a Jewish publican on contract with the Roman government. The Romans controlled an immense expanse of territory and levied taxes on all nations in their vast empire. Subjects under Roman rule were required to pay a tax when they moved their goods to a market outside their immediate territory. The tariff wiped out most of the profits they had earned.

The Roman government outsourced the extortion efforts to publicans, or chief tax collectors. Publicans were required to deposit the prescribed amount of taxes in the treasury, but they and their staff of tax collectors were free to shake down citizens for "bonus taxes" to enhance their share of the take. Accordingly, tax collectors typically perpetrated despicable acts in the extortion. Tax collectors, therefore, were universally despised because farmers and business owners frequently spiraled to destitution because of the tax collectors' fraudulent practices.[13]

Most likely, Zacchaeus was particularly loathed because he lived in Jericho, a rich and flourishing town about seventeen miles north of Jerusalem. Its warm climate contributed to a thriving agricultural trade in the region. Jericho was also the border city between the provinces of Judea and Perea, so its thriving import-export market enhanced Zacchaeus's seedy career.

Zacchaeus lived in an upscale part of the city, opulent perhaps, by first-century standards. The ruler, Herod, even maintained a vast winter palace there, with sumptuous ornamental gardens.[14] The air was fragrant with the fullness of the lush countryside. In fact, Jericho was celebrated for the palm trees that adorned the plain around the city.

Wrath toward tax collectors was universal, but the Jews in particular had an additional bone to pick with them. Jews were opposed to the taxes because the money went to support the pagan Roman government. Tax collectors of Jewish heritage, such as Zacchaeus, were considered traitors because they allied themselves with the Roman oppressors, and they gouged their fellow Jews to line their own pockets. And tax collectors, because of their frequent contact with Gentiles, or non-Jews, were considered ritually unclean. Rabbis cautioned their pupils not to eat with such persons. For these reasons, Scripture often refers to tax collectors as sordid individuals. Often they are lumped with sinners in general.

So, although Zacchaeus was a man of considerable wealth, his wealth came with a high price. He was a social outcast, scorned by all but his fellow tax collectors.

Enter Jesus, friend of the sinful and the scorned.

Early in His public ministry, Jesus caused a scandal by seeking out these unsavory types. One of the first disciples He invited to follow Him was an undesirable named Matthew. Jesus saw Matthew sitting at his tax collector's booth and extended an invitation, "Follow Me." To the religious leaders, this was heresy. To the Jews earnestly trying to live a devout life, this was troublesome. But to Matthew, wow! He was *chosen.* He was accepted, included, and befriended.

Matthew left his counting table and followed Jesus straightaway. He held a party at his home in Jesus' honor. Whom did he invite to the bash? Why, his friends, of course. Who were his friends? Other social outcasts—his fellow tax collectors. Sinners.

Think of someone you greatly admire for his or her virtuous qualities, perhaps a religious figure or social activist. Now imagine that you viewed a clip on YouTube of that person having dinner at the home of a local drug lord. The reaction of the Pharisees, considered the holiest of religious leaders of the time, was similar. Hearing about Jesus' scandalous behavior, they asked His disciples, "Why does your teacher party with tax collectors and sinners?"[15]

Did Jesus feel busted? Did He call a press conference to vindicate Himself? Did He say that He regretted His unwitting association with the scum of society? Hardly. Jesus made it clear that He deliberately sought the company of these sinners. Jesus told the Pharisees, "It is not the healthy who need a doctor, but the sick. I have not come to call the righteous, but sinners to repentance."[16] Like Garth Brooks, Jesus openly boasted that He had friends in low places.

Denouncing pretense and self-aggrandizement, Jesus repeatedly chose to befriend those who were castoffs. And He didn't just tolerate these sinners. He *liked* them. The self-righteous Pharisees called Him on it again and again. They seethed when Jesus denigrated them—the mighty, pious "Keepers of the Law." They were outraged when Jesus preached, "don't be like them," as He traveled throughout Palestine talking to the masses.

During His travels, Jesus often spoke to the people in parables, short fictitious stories used to drive home a point. Jesus was a master storyteller, and His stories always resonated with His audience. Many times He used the parables to challenge the religious leaders, contrasting them with tax collectors, Samaritans, and other outcasts. In each instance, the social derelict emerged as the good guy while the true, vile, arrogant nature of the self-righteous was exposed.

In one such parable Jesus told of two men, a Pharisee and a tax collector, who went to the temple to pray. The Pharisee touted his own good deeds and uttered a prayer of thanks that he was not like the tax collectors and sinners. By contrast, the tax collector stood at a distance from the temple, too ashamed to even look up to heaven. He beat his breast and from his earnest, repentant heart cried out, "God have mercy on me, a sinner."[17] In telling this story, Jesus conveyed to those within earshot that it was the tax collector, not the religious man, who was thereby justified before God: "for all those who exalt themselves will be humbled, and those who humble themselves will be exalted."

This was an astonishing reversal of cultural norms. Many of those who heard Jesus were gripped by His message and sought Him out. The masses adored Him; the religious elite hated Him. But love Him or hate Him, *everyone* was fascinated with Him.

No doubt Zacchaeus had heard of Jesus' fame. Certainly he'd heard that Jesus was befriending tax collectors and sinners. Perhaps Zacchaeus was enthralled by Jesus' merciful nature. It's likely that he knew someone who had dined with Jesus at Matthew's home, the tax collector from Capernaum, at the opposite end of the Jordan River. Regardless of how he came to know of Jesus, Zacchaeus, this vile sinner, was determined to see Him.

Jesus was traveling from the Jordan River to Jerusalem, a trip that would end in His arrest and execution. For the past three years, His popularity had been mushrooming and, by that time, swarms of followers accompanied Him everywhere He went.

When Zacchaeus heard that Jesus was passing by, he rushed to catch a glimpse of the famous teacher. But a multitude of people had already gathered along the path. Being short of stature, Zacchaeus couldn't see above the heads of the other followers. His zeal undaunted, Zacchaeus spotted a sycamore-fig tree along the path in the direction Jesus was headed. This particular variety of tree has many limbs that begin just a few feet from the ground, which made climbing easy, even for a short man.[18] With no time to spare and nothing but his pride to lose, Zacchaeus scrambled up the tree, intent on catching a glimpse of Jesus, the friend of sinners.

Those who spotted Zacchaeus must have thought he looked like an utter fool. A grown man, wealthy and clad with all his finery, clambering up a tree. Did they taunt him? Maybe someone shouted, "Zacchaeus, Ha! All your wealth can't buy you a ticket to the front line of this parade!" No, his wealth couldn't score him a ticket to meet the Master, but his zeal could. His sincerity could. His repentant heart could.

Jesus spied Zacchaeus high in the tree, above the heads of the others in the crowd. I imagine Him laughing heartily as He spotted the tax collector crouching in the tree like a playful monkey. "Scurry on down here, Zacchaeus! I *must* stay at your house today."

Spend some time with Jesus—get to know Him, bask in His love—and something profound is bound to happen to your heart. Zacchaeus was wrenched with conviction, compelled to turn away from his sinful ways. His confession to his houseguest was ambitious and sincere: "Here and now I give half of my possessions to the poor, and if I have cheated anybody out of anything, I will pay back four times the amount."

Jesus said to him, "Today salvation has come to this house, because this man, too, is a son of Abraham. For the Son of Man came to seek and to save the lost."

Salvation. It's a lofty word, right? It refers to deliverance from the power and effects of sin.[19] Jesus used this same word when He spoke with the Samaritan woman at the well. "Salvation is from the Jews," He told her. About two thousand years earlier, God made an eternity-altering promise to an old man named Abraham.[20] Despite the fact that Abraham and his wife were far past the age to have children, God promised him that he would have countless descendants. He pledged that through Abraham He would build a great nation, and that all nations would be blessed through Abraham, through his offspring.

As the offspring of Abraham, the Jews were the nation of the promise—the people through whom all nations would be blessed. They viewed it as the highest possible status. But because of the profession Zacchaeus had chosen, he wasn't simply a social outcast. He had been excommunicated from the synagogue and had forfeited his birthright as a son of Abraham. Surely the banishment gnawed at Zacchaeus every day of his life.

With uncanny sensitivity and grace, Jesus chose to publicly reinstate Zacchaeus's status as "a son of Abraham." To the dismay of those in the crowd, He restored Zacchaeus to the people with whom God initially made His covenant, the esteemed chosen nation. Jesus declared that because Zacchaeus had earnestly sought the true Son of God and because he had repented, he was truly free. Jesus lifted Zacchaeus from a very low place and befriended him.

There are many people I admire greatly. We all have our heroes. Who is it for you? An actor or a musician? A political leader or a social activist? An author or a poet?

Recently my husband, Steve, and I attended a Paul McCartney concert in Chicago, not far from our home. We didn't have great seats. They were at least one hundred rows back, but we were able to see the Beatles legend and counted ourselves lucky just to be there. What if he had spotted us way back there and announced he wanted to spend the evening in our home? In that fantasy, I am flabbergasted and can hardly believe my good fortune! He picked *me*! He's coming to stay at *my* house!

That's the kind of reaction—multiplied by ten thousand—that Zacchaeus experienced when Jesus picked him. Because Jesus was not just a celebrity. He wasn't admired for His musical or acting talent. He wasn't esteemed simply for His leadership or social activism. He wasn't famous because of His writing or poetic skills. *This man was transforming people from the inside out.* And likewise, He transformed Zacchaeus.

Basking in Jesus' love light, Zacchaeus's sin was revealed—as repugnant and hideous as it was. In an instant, Zacchaeus could no longer endure his wicked ways, and he turned from them to face the glorious radiance of the Friend of Sinners.

No one but Jesus can elicit a transformation like that. Not Paul McCartney or Taylor Swift. Not Brad Pitt or Kristen Stewart. Not Nelson Mandela or Oprah. Only Jesus can bring forth the kind of change that erases the sins of the repentant, heals a lonely heart, and transforms a soul.

In quiet moments, I reflect on my sinful nature. I think of all the times I've treasured my belongings, been unkind to those I love, or failed to make time for those in need—puffed up with pride and self-absorption. In these times, I am filled with shame and, like the tax collector in the parable, my repentant heart cries out, "God, have mercy on me, a sinner." In this humble state I know for sure I am pitifully unworthy to approach a holy and omnipotent God. But soon my soul is filled with joy as I remember the lesson of Zacchaeus, and it is this: Jesus adores me. He has friends in low places.

Out of the depths
I cry to you, LORD;
Lord, hear my voice.
Let your ears be attentive to my cry for mercy.
Psalm 130:1-2

Can You Relate?

Questions for Personal Reflection or Group Discussion

1. Think of someone with whom you avoid interacting because of the profession or the lifestyle they have chosen.

    a. What profession or lifestyle does this person have?

    _____

    _____

    b. Why are you reluctant to interact with this person?

    _____

    _____

    c. Do you feel you are superior to this person? If so, why?

    _____

    _____

2. Reflect on a time when you or someone you love was shunned because of profession or lifestyle. Share this, if you choose, with the group, including how you felt.

    _____

    _____

3. Has there been a time when you chose to befriend or interact with someone whom others shunned due to their profession or lifestyle? If so, share what led you to engage that person. How did that interaction affect you?

    _____

    _____

4. Think of someone who regularly seeks to befriend people with a seedy lifestyle or profession. How do you feel about this?

_____

_____

5. Jesus befriended Zacchaeus, a man in a "low place." How do you think Jesus feels about you when you are in a "low place"?

_____

_____

6. As you reflect on Jesus' encounter with Zacchaeus, which of Jesus' traits stand out?

_____

_____

CHAPTER 6

Jesus Visits Martha and Mary

As Jesus and his disciples were on their way, he came to a village where a woman named Martha opened her home to him. She had a sister called Mary, who sat at the Lord's feet listening to what he said. But Martha was distracted by all the preparations that had to be made. She came to him and asked, "Lord, don't you care that my sister has left me to do the work by myself? Tell her to help me!"

"Martha, Martha," the Lord answered, "you are worried and upset about many things, but few things are needed—or indeed only one. Mary has chosen what is better, and it will not be taken away from her."

Luke10:38-42

Direction for the Distracted

Martha had spunk. It's one of the things I admire about her. Scripture tells us, "Jesus loved Martha and her sister and Lazarus."[21] They lived in Bethany, a couple of miles from Jerusalem, the city of the temple. The home belonged to Martha. Her siblings, Mary and Lazarus, lived with her. Because Martha had a home but was not married, she was probably a widow.

On this particular visit to Bethany, Jesus and His disciples were visiting Martha and her siblings. Martha busied herself getting everything just right for her special guests. It's not clear from Scripture whether Lazarus and Jesus' disciples were in the home at the time of our story or whether they were away. They are not specifically mentioned in this story, but all of them would surely be present for dinner, so Martha was preparing a meal for the whole crowd.

While Martha worked, Mary sat with Jesus, listening to Him speak. Martha fumed that her younger sister wasn't helping her.

Did Martha have a valid point? A meal did need to be prepared, right? She couldn't just call Pizza Hut and order four large thin crust pepperoni pizzas and a bucket of wings.

The story generates a litany of questions in my mind: Why was Mary so insensitive to Martha's tasks? Didn't she understand just how much work it takes to throw a dinner party? Shouldn't she have been helping Martha? Was she just lazy? Why didn't Jesus support Martha and send Mary to help her sister?

Then I thought of Mom.

We all knew she wouldn't be with us much longer. Lung disease had robbed my mother of her former spunk and exuberance. She and Dad still lived in the home my siblings and I had grown up in. Dad was doing all right, but he was in his eighties. The demands of taking care of his ailing wife, doing laundry, and keeping a clean home were daunting.

My business afforded me some flexibility with my schedule, so in those days, I took off every Friday and drove the twenty miles to spend the day with my parents. I looked forward to seeing them all week. I also recognized that being able to set aside this treasured day was a blessing not every adult child is given.

In preparation for my Friday visit, I always pondered what I could do that would make life a little easier for my parents. I often stopped to buy groceries, relieving Dad of that task. And before my trip, I prepared to-do lists: Change the batteries in the smoke detectors. Replace the furnace filter. Scrub the kitchen floor. Clean the bathroom. Prepare dinner. Change the bed linens. Take out the garbage.

Each week I'd spurt through the door, give each parent a kiss, talk for a bit, and then hit the ground running. So much to do. So little time before I had to head for home, greet my kids as they arrived from school, and prepare dinner for my family.

My parents appreciated everything I did for them. I knew that. Maybe that's why I was taken aback at my mother's admonition during one of my visits. I remember it vividly. "Sue, will you *please sit down*?"

"But Mom, there's so much still to do, and I have only one more hour until I have to head home."

"Exactly. So sit down and talk to me."

I was torn. Of course, I longed to sit and talk with my mother. I loved her fiercely. How much longer would we have her? Clearly, her health was failing dramatically. But oh, there was so very much to do.

On subsequent visits, I sometimes remembered her admonishment, so I sat and talked with her for longer periods of time. Looking back, though, I realize we seldom had heart-to-heart talks in those days. I was distracted by many things and, therefore, didn't make time for such luxuries.

Several hospital emergencies followed over the next year. Mom became weaker and frailer each week. Surely she knew her death was imminent. Her focus shifted from seeking healing to ensuring the well-being of her family after her departure.

Oh, the anguish we all felt as we faced the looming inevitability of her death. After returning from her latest hospital stay, she was lethargic and bedridden, and under hospice care. We rented a hospital bed and placed it in the living room so she wouldn't be confined to her bedroom. Being in the living room allowed her to experience some of the bustle of life, and it accommodated the steady stream of loved ones coming to see her.

In the last few weeks of her life, she had a live-in caretaker, in addition to my eight siblings and me, who took turns being with her around the clock. One frigid February day, I had the early morning shift with Mom. When I arrived she was sleeping soundly, her breathing made easier by the oxygen delivered via tube. "Good morning, Mom. It's Sue. I'm here. I love you." No response. Just peaceful sleep. I took comfort in the steady rise and fall of her chest and her rhythmic shallow breathing.

The window behind Mom's bed was bare. I had thought it would be pleasant to hang a set of curtains, which would block out the sunlight and help her to rest more comfortably. I had chosen a cheerful flowery design for the curtains and brought them with me that morning. They just needed a quick touchup with the iron, and they'd be ready to hang.

I left Mom in the capable hands of her caretaker, ran down the stairs to the basement and quickly ironed the panels. I then scurried back upstairs, excusing her caretaker for some essential rest. Dad had already gone to take a much-needed nap. I headed to the living room, climbed a stepstool, swiftly hung the curtains, and stepped back to admire them. The sun was just beginning to rise and a soft beam of light peeked through the sheer curtains. Beautiful, I thought. Then I glanced at Mom to check on her. The oxygen tube was no longer in her nose; it was dangling near her face. "Mom!" I cried. But there was no response. And I knew.

Oh, what a precious mother I had. I grieved her death for a long while. I missed everything about her. Her smile. The burning love she had for me and for, well, everyone. In my whole life, no one would ever love me like my mom did. I longed to hold her, to smell her freshly shampooed hair and the earthy scent of her skin from the sesame oil she had used daily. I yearned for the sound of her voice. I missed the songs she had sung. I ached for her phone calls. But eventually, healing came. Happiness returned to my life, and I could laugh again.

One day, a year or so after her death, I was enjoying a sunny Sunday afternoon with my husband. We were making the rounds of some home improvement stores, looking for some repair items. The car radio was on and I was singing along with the tunes. Then a particular song came on the radio. It was a rather obscure boy-loses-girl song by Billy Vera and the Beaters. I'd heard it many times, but this time I heard the words with the ears of a lost child aching for her mother's caress: "What do you think I would give at this moment? If you'd stay I'd subtract twenty years from my life. I'd fall down on my knees, kiss the ground that you walk on, if I could just hold you again."[22]

The rest of the world disappeared, and I was drenched in grief. In an instant I found myself sobbing, drowning in a pool of tears. "Oh Mom, if I could just hold you again! Twenty years. I'd subtract *twenty years* from my life."

Steve pulled the car off the road, parked, and held me tight. "She wouldn't let you. She wouldn't let you give up *one day* of your life. She loved you too much."

In the years since Mom's death, I have reflected on my own Martha-ness many, many times. I don't regret the things that I did for Mom, but I do regret that I didn't spend more time just *being* with her. Surely, I should have chosen what was better. How I wished I had heard more stories and asked for more guidance. How I lament that I wasn't holding her hand instead of holding up curtains as she passed from this world into God's presence. Only one thing was needed, but I hadn't chosen it.

Imagine stepping into Martha and Mary's living room. Jesus sits on the couch. Mary is at His feet, a posture used to honor a welcome guest. She's enthralled with Him. She delights in His stories and gladly receives His guidance about many important things. Jesus feels welcome and loved. Mary relishes these moments. She's smitten by Jesus as were the Samaritan woman at the well, Zacchaeus, and countless others who followed Him. His tenderness and mercy draw her in, and she can't bear to leave His presence.

In walks Martha, complaining to her guest as she observes her sister dawdling with unimportant matters. "Make her help me," she implores.

And you know, I understand Martha's frustration. Even with all of the modern kitchen conveniences, entertaining can be *hard* work. But here's Martha, complaining to her guest that His presence is causing her a lot of work and that she could really use a hand. Jesus' response exudes His love. He assures Martha that an elaborate spread is not needed. Lentils and rice would suffice. What Jesus really longed for was her *presence.*

His reply is so full of love for both Martha and Mary. Can't you just hear it? "Martha, Martha. You are worried and upset about many things, but few things are needed—or indeed only one. Mary has chosen what is better, and it will not be taken from her."

It's uncanny how Jesus' words spoken to a friend twenty centuries ago stretch through the ages and across the continents to my heart in my suburban Chicago town. His words are no less relevant now than when He first spoke them. With unfailing love and a mighty vision of the life He longs for me to have, I hear Him speak to me deep within my heart: "Sue, Sue, you are distracted by many things. Only one thing is needed. Choose what is better. It will not be taken from you."

*Let the message of Christ dwell among you richly as you teach
and admonish one another with all wisdom through psalms,
hymns and songs from the Spirit, singing to God with gratitude
in your hearts.*
Colossians 3:16

Can You Relate?

Questions for Personal Reflection or Group Discussion

1. Jesus was a close friend of Lazarus and his sisters, Martha and Mary. Scripture tells us that He loved each of them.

    a. Think of someone you know and like who has personality traits similar to Martha. What is it that you like about this person?

    _____

    _____

    b. Think of someone you know and like with personality traits similar to Mary. What is it that you like about this person?

    _____

    _____

2. Jesus said Mary had chosen what was "better," and it would not be taken from her. What do you think He meant by that?

    _____

    _____

3. How do you imagine Martha reacted when Jesus told her Mary had chosen what was better?

    _____

    _____

4. Reflect on a time when someone worked hard as a favor to you. What impact did their actions have on you?

    _____

    _____

5. Think of a time when someone sat and talked with you at length, reflecting on you and your needs and interests. What impact did that encounter have on you?

    _____

    _____

6. Share, if you choose, a time when you didn't choose what was better, a choice you now regret.

    _____

    _____

7. In general, what things distract you from choosing what is better?

    _____

    _____

8. Consider how you can minimize some of the distractions in your life and begin to choose more of what is better. Share your thoughts with the group, if you choose.

    _____

    _____

CHAPTER 7

Jesus Defends a Sinful Woman

When one of the Pharisees invited Jesus to have dinner with him, he went to the Pharisee's house and reclined at the table. A woman in that town who lived a sinful life learned that Jesus was eating at the Pharisee's house, so she came there with an alabaster jar of perfume. As she stood behind him at his feet weeping, she began to wet his feet with her tears. Then she wiped them with her hair, kissed them and poured perfume on them.

When the Pharisee who had invited him saw this, he said to himself, "If this man were a prophet, he would know who is touching him and what kind of woman she is—that she is a sinner."

Jesus answered him, "Simon, I have something to tell you."

"Tell me, teacher," he said.

"Two people owed money to a certain moneylender. One owed him five hundred denarii, and the other fifty. Neither of them had the money to pay him back, so he forgave the debts of both. Now which of them will love him more?"

Simon replied, "I suppose the one who had the bigger debt forgiven."

"You have judged correctly," Jesus said.

Then he turned toward the woman and said to Simon, "Do you see this woman? I came into your house. You did not give me any water for my feet, but she wet my feet with her tears and wiped them with her hair. You did not give me a kiss, but this woman, from the time I entered, has not stopped kissing my feet. You did not put oil on my head, but she has poured perfume on my feet. Therefore, I tell you, her many sins have been forgiven—as her great love has shown. But whoever has been forgiven little loves little."

Then Jesus said to her, "Your sins are forgiven."

The other guests began to say among themselves, "Who is this who even forgives sins?"

Jesus said to the woman, "Your faith has saved you; go in peace."

Luke 7:36-50

Impartially Merciful

When will He ever learn? Once again, we see Jesus hanging with a loser. This time, it's a woman of ill repute. He was offered numerous chances to hang out with the good people. This scriptural account shows us yet another of those opportunities. He'd been invited to dine with an important man. A respected man. A religious man. And Jesus graciously accepted the invitation.

Why did Simon extend the invitation to Jesus? Were his intentions genuine? Did he want to get to know Him better? By now, Jesus was well known throughout the region. He'd been to Bethany, a small town near Jerusalem, several times. He'd preached in the synagogues, at the temple, and on the mountainside. He'd healed the sick and bestowed hope upon the poor and the meek. Jesus' disdain for pretention, particularly religious pretention, was well known. Still, Simon, a Pharisee educated in the sacred writings of the Jews, invited Jesus to his home. Throughout the New Testament accounts, Jesus interacts with Pharisees again and again. So what's up with these Pharisees?

They were one of the three groups of Jewish leaders in first-century Palestine. These men were serious students of Jewish Scripture, treasured as sacred. The Pharisees stood out among others as being devoted to the laws contained in these documents. They were, in fact, so dedicated to them that they established a massive set of supplemental oral laws, initially designed to interpret Holy Scripture. But soon, the supplemental laws of the

Pharisees were deemed as holy as the original sacred writings. Further, the Pharisees claimed that their adherence to both the scriptural laws and their homegrown bonus laws entitled them to a certain level of esteem. And esteemed they were. They were held in high regard as they set about to do many good, godly things. They were devoted to ceremonial washings and public fasting, and they gave a tenth of all their income to the synagogue or temple.

Those are all *good* things, right? So why did Jesus repeatedly clash with the Pharisees?

Throughout Scripture, this is abundantly clear: God sees us on the inside. Our outward acts by themselves do not impress God. He is concerned with the condition of our hearts. Unless motivated by love alone, all our good works lack merit. Without love, our good works serve only our own selfish motives. We cannot hide the condition of our hearts from God.

Paul was a Pharisee who turned away from his pride, believed the message that Jesus delivered, and became a fervent follower of Jesus. In a letter to the Corinthians, Paul explained God's perspective on the relation between what we do and why we do it:

> If I speak in the tongues of men or of angels, but
> do not have love, I am only a resounding gong or a
> clanging cymbal. If I have the gift of prophecy and
> can fathom all mysteries and all knowledge, and if
> I have a faith that can move mountains, but do not
> have love, I am nothing. If I give all I possess to the
> poor and give over my body to hardship that I may
> boast, but do not have love, I gain nothing.
>
> Love is patient, love is kind. It does not envy, it
> does not boast, it is not proud. It does not dishonor

others, it is not self-seeking, it is not easily angered,
it keeps no record of wrongs. Love does not delight
in evil but rejoices with the truth. It always protects,
always trusts, always hopes, always perseveres. Love
never fails.

And now these three remain: faith, hope and love.
But the greatest of these is love.[23]

The Pharisees did a lot of good things, but few, if any, of their
acts were motivated by love. They were like clanging symbols.
On at least three occasions, Jesus graciously accepted invitations
to dine with Pharisees.[24] He loved them and longed to extend
salvation to each of them. He yearned for them to experience the
freedom that would come when they realized there was nothing
they could do to earn their salvation. He offered a gift, the only
gift that could outlast the grave, but most Pharisees shunned the
gift. They were too haughty. They refused to humble themselves
and to acknowledge their outward acts were worthless. Each
of them was essentially his own god. How could they accept a
Savior if they couldn't recognize their need for one?

What happened at Simon's house illustrates the Pharisees'
inability to see their sinfulness. Why had Simon invited Jesus?
He didn't even show Jesus the common courtesies of the day.
Since most people traveled by foot on dusty, unpaved roads, it
was customary to offer a guest some water to refresh their feet.
But Simon didn't do that. Hosts also anointed a guest's head
with a bit of oil—not with expensive oil, just common olive oil.
It was a gesture of hospitality and respect.[25] But Simon failed to
do that as well. Jesus overlooked these omissions and reclined at
Simon's table. (Tables were low to the ground, so people reclined
at the table with their legs to the side, knees bent.)

Such receptions for visiting guests were open to the public; anyone was welcome to come.[26] Any *man* was welcome to come, that is. Not women. And certainly not *sinful* women.

But this particular woman came. Why had she come? Jesus had been traveling throughout the area healing the sick and teaching the crowds. He spoke of the great love God has for the lowly. "Blessed are those who weep now," He told them, "for they will laugh."[27]

Had this woman been in the crowd? Had she heard His words with her ears and responded with her heart? Had she been drenched in the love Jesus gave away so freely?

Risking rejection by the religious elite, she entered the dinner reception. She knew the important people in attendance would criticize her, but Jesus had transformed her life. She just had to thank Him. She was keenly aware of the gravity of her sin, yet more keenly aware of Jesus' love. In her heart, she knew He was the Messiah sent by God to rescue His people and to bring respite to her battered soul. Compelled by faith, she took on the posture of a servant, slightly behind Jesus and at His feet. Merely being in His presence made her cry. Her tears fell freely onto His soiled feet. Having no towel to offer, she dried them with her hair.

And she brought with her the only gift she had. Perhaps she'd received it as compensation for the tawdry acts she had engaged in. All that was behind her now. She didn't hold back what she was able to give. In gratitude, she broke the jar and poured the fragrant oil, every last drop of it, on the head of her Messiah. She gave what she had. She did what she could.

In the summer of 1989, my family and I spent a week in San Francisco. Our children were young at the time—Michael was six and Stacey was three. They delighted in the sights and sounds of the misty city by the bay. Each morning, we left our hotel in an "affordable" section of the city and walked a mile or so to the cable cars, which took us to our destination for the day. We drank in the character of the city. Each building seemed to tell a story of past residents. Each winding street promised a new adventure. The Oakland Bay Bridge fascinated us—its miles of suspended concrete overlooking the San Francisco Bay.

One thing that disturbed us was the large homeless population huddled alongside the buildings we passed each morning and evening as we walked to and from the cable cars. We learned that the moderate temperatures of the Bay area drew an increasingly burgeoning homeless population. Nighttime frequently brought chilly temperatures that remained until the sun rose to warm the city once again. On our morning walks to the cable cars, many homeless people were crowded against the buildings with their plastic bags of treasured, meager belongings: a pair of tattered socks, a can of Spam, a battered book, or a picture of a loved one. The faces of these unkempt people were dirty and rugged. Their eyes held no hope as they approached us, asking if we could spare a quarter or perhaps a dollar.

I'm ashamed to say that, although I pitied these people, a part of me found them an annoying distraction from a vacation our family had anticipated all year. They spoiled the blissful mood that otherwise enveloped us as we enjoyed our family togetherness.

On the final night of our vacation, after exiting the cable car, we stopped at a fast food restaurant a couple of blocks from our hotel. As we sat at the table eating burgers and fries, we reminisced about our vacation adventures and spoke excitedly about our return home the following morning. As we talked, we noticed a man at a nearby table. We'd seen him before—leaning against a building beside his bag of belongings, a vacant hopelessness in his eyes. Now he was sitting in the fast food restaurant, drinking a cup of coffee and warming his cold, tired bones. Alone.

As we were about to leave, this man with the rugged, unshaven face approached our table. "Pardon me," he said. "I've seen you before. I've watched you on your morning walks. You have such a beautiful family. I hope you'll accept this gift from me." He placed a slip of paper in my husband's palm and walked away. We all thanked him hastily as he ambled outside into the chill of the night. Steve opened his palm to reveal what this man had blessed us with. It was a coupon for a free breakfast sandwich at the fast food restaurant where we were sitting. This was his gift.

We weren't able to use the coupon. We left early the next morning, heading straight to the airport. We weren't wealthy people, but we always had money for food, and we never had to miss a meal. For that man, though, a coupon for a free breakfast sandwich had great value. Perhaps he had no meal the following morning because he had given it to us. He had almost nothing, but what he did have, he gave away. He gave it freely to the strangers he'd seen walking in the mornings en route to the cable cars that took us places he could only dream of going. My family and I believe he was motivated only by love. He couldn't do much. But he did what he could.

At Simon's home, Jesus spoke these words: "Her many sins have been forgiven—as her great love has shown. But whoever has been forgiven little loves little." Jesus' pronouncement extended forgiveness to the woman and conviction to Simon.

Jesus' words convict me as well. Each of us has amassed a huge pile of sin we drag through life. I've learned that the closer I walk with God, the more aware I am of my sinful nature and the large debt that has been canceled by Jesus' death on the cross. The better I know Jesus, the less I identify with the upstanding Pharisees who did many good deeds. I now identify more with the sinful woman with the alabaster jar. I feel compelled to sit at my Savior's feet and to offer all I have. I want to do what I can, because I love much.

Each of you should give what you have decided in your heart to give, not reluctantly or under compulsion, for God loves a cheerful giver.
2 Corinthians 9:7

Can You Relate?

Questions for Personal Reflection or Group Discussion

1. The sinful woman gifted Jesus with the alabaster jar of perfume. The homeless man gifted Sue's family with the coupon for a free breakfast sandwich. Have you ever been given a gift that has similarly blown you away? If so, what was it and why was it so special?

   _____

   _____

2. Despite the often-contentious interactions between Jesus and the Pharisees, Jesus accepted invitations to dine with Pharisees on at least three occasions. Why do you think He chose to accept their invitations?

   _____

   _____

3. Why do you think that Jesus selected the parable of the moneylender to share with Simon?

   _____

   _____

4. Considering the story of Jesus and the woman with the alabaster jar, what is necessary for a person's sins to be forgiven: faith, love, or something else?

   _____

   _____

5. How does the parable of the moneylender relate to your life?

_____

_____

6. The people at Simon's house were astonished when Jesus told the woman her sins were forgiven. They asked, "Who is this who even forgives sins?" Why were they so astonished?

_____

_____

7. How do you think the woman at Simon's house felt when Jesus told her that her sins were forgiven?

_____

_____

CHAPTER 8

Jesus Forgives the Repentant Criminal

Two other men, both criminals, were also led out with him to be executed. When they came to the place called the Skull, they crucified him there, along with the criminals—one on his right, the other on his left. Jesus said, "Father, forgive them, for they do not know what they are doing." And they divided up his clothes by casting lots.

The people stood watching, and the rulers even sneered at him. They said, "He saved others; let him save himself if he is God's Messiah, the Chosen One."

The soldiers also came up and mocked him. They offered him wine vinegar and said, "If you are the king of the Jews, save yourself."

There was a written notice above him, which read: THIS IS THE KING OF THE JEWS.

One of the criminals who hung there hurled insults at him: "Aren't you the Messiah? Save yourself and us!"

But the other criminal rebuked him. "Don't you fear God," he said, "since you are under the same sentence? We are punished justly, for we are getting what our deeds deserve. But this man has done nothing wrong."

Then he said, "Jesus, remember me when you come into your kingdom."

Jesus answered him, "Truly I tell you, today you will be with me in paradise."

Luke 23:32-43

84

Savior of Sinners

Three years. That's how long Jesus had been a public figure. Thirty years of lower middle-class obscurity followed by three years of building a foundation for what would become the most audacious movement ever to rock planet Earth. Nobody in history has had such a profound impact on mankind as this one man. And it all started with a three-year not-for-profit gig.

The plan was beautiful in its simplicity.

First, recruit a group of leaders. Twelve was the perfect number—small enough to establish real intimacy yet large enough to launch an enormous movement.

Second, teach the people. Teach at the synagogues, speak on the seashore, preach on the mountainsides. Tell the people about the extraordinary, tender love of a God who invites us to call Him *Abba*, Father. Explain that they are to serve one another, that they are strongest when they are weak, and that they are blessed when they are meek.

Third, demonstrate His deity. The people needed proof that Jesus was more than a kind man, more than a brilliant theologian. He would perform miracles: Turn water into wine. Walk on water. Multiply a few loaves of bread to feed thousands. Heal the sick. Raise the dead.

Fourth, submit. Submit to the will of the heavenly Father who had sent Him. Submit to the persecution of the religious leaders. Yield to the Roman rulers' death sentence. Accept the abandonment of His closest friends. Endure unimaginable agony as He was stripped, whipped, punched, and pierced. Be obedient to death—even death on a cross.

On that tree Jesus would hang for three hours. Bludgeoned and bloodied. But in those dark hours, He would continue to teach, to demonstrate the breadth of His love for *all* people, and to offer solace and forgiveness of sins.

It began on a Thursday. The great Passover Feast. Jews had been celebrating this holy feast annually for well over 1400 years. It commemorated the night God passed over His people, protecting them from harm as He pronounced judgment on Egypt for Pharaoh's relentless refusal to free the Hebrew people from bondage. The demonstration of God's hand in the first Passover was so dramatic and so devastating that Pharaoh finally permitted the Hebrews to leave the Egyptian territory, thus making it possible for them to become a free nation. As God had instructed them, the Jews observed the event with an annual ceremonial meal celebrated with loved ones.

Jesus knew this particular Passover supper would be His last meal before His crucifixion. His suffering was at hand. In just a few hours, He would be arrested and the torturous road to the cross would ensue.

Jesus, the great lover until the end, took on the role of a servant at the meal. The great master and teacher stooped to the ground to wash the filthy feet of His friends. When He had finished He told them, "I have set you an example that you should do as I have done for you . . . Now that you know these things, you will be blessed if you do them."[28]

As they broke the bread and shared the wine to celebrate Passover, Jesus told them that they should do likewise to commemorate the sacrifice He was about to offer. His body would be broken and His blood would be spilled. Just as God had commanded His people to carefully commemorate the Passover, Jesus was now commanding His followers to observe His suffering on their behalf. Some things are too important to ever forget.

When they had finished the meal, Jesus took His followers to a place where He prayed. "My soul is overwhelmed with sorrow to the point of death. Stay here and keep watch with me."[29] But while Jesus prayed to His heavenly Father, asking if there might be another way to fulfill His mission, His friends fell asleep. Jesus returned to His Father again in prayer, "Not as I will, but as you will."[30]

And with that, His tormentors came to arrest Him. Thousands of books have been written on the events that followed. Each detail of the Passion Story provides insight into Jesus and God the Father. Each iota is resplendent with a divine love.

The crux of the story is this: the love of God the Father and of Jesus the Son never fails.

The two criminals who died alongside Jesus hold profound relevance for our lives. Envision Jesus in *this* setting. It is a vivid contrast to the scenes of Jesus talking quietly with the Samaritan woman at the well, teaching the masses on the mountainside, or entering Jericho to the hails of jubilant crowds.

In this scene, Jesus is nailed to a cross. He is naked except for a crown of thorns that has been ground into His head. He has gaping wounds on His back from the brutal whipping He has endured. The skin is ripped from His torso. His face is barely recognizable because of the repeated beatings He has received. He is parched and dehydrated; He hasn't had even a sip of water. There is blood. So much blood.

Beside Him hang two criminals. Their crimes are grievous. The Bible says they were robbers—not thieves in the night. The wording indicates that they likely committed acts of violence as they pilfered the money and belongings of their victims.[31] One of the criminals even admits they deserve the punishment they have received.

Like Jesus, they hang naked on their crosses—a hideous punishment, reserved for the most treacherous criminals. As the three hang together on the erected planks, the religious leaders and the crowd mock Jesus. "He saved others," they say, "but he can't save himself!" Initially both of the criminals hanging beside Jesus join in the heckling. "Aren't you the Messiah? Save yourself and us."

Both criminals listen to Jesus—now barely alive and reduced to a mass of pulp. One of the criminals, though, pays attention while He hangs beside Jesus. He hears Jesus beg God to forgive the people who had tortured Him: "Father forgive them, for they do not know what they are doing."

One criminal remains untouched by Jesus' words. He taunts the Savior, intent on wallowing in his sin. Firm in his resolve to die as he had lived—utterly apart from God.

The man hanging at Jesus' other side had committed the same crimes as his cohort. He too was notorious. He too had lived a life far from God. But this man, in the midst of his suffering, in the hour of his death, recognizes that the man hanging beside Him is no mere man. In the words of forgiveness Jesus murmured, this man recognizes the voice of God. *Truly this man is sinless*, he thinks. *He surely is a king and His kingdom will outlast this life. Even at the hour of His death, He asked God to forgive His crucifiers. If He will forgive them, He will forgive even a wretch like me.*

"Jesus, remember me when you come into your kingdom."

And then this wretched criminal hears some of the last words that Jesus speaks before His death: "Truly I tell you, today you will be with me in paradise."

How I loved my father-in-law. From the moment we met when I was seventeen, he was gracious to me. I learned that he had always been a devoted father to my husband and that he loved his stepsons as if they were simply sons. And despite their comic bantering, he was a dedicated husband to his wife, Ann. He was adored by all of the Ciullo clan: his siblings and in-laws, nieces and nephews. At his wake, one of his nephews opined, "Uncle Mike was the most charming of all of the uncles." It was a fitting tribute.[32]

He was a war hero too—although he never mentioned it. His brothers and friends, fellow WWII vets, told us. He was a radio engineer in the US Army Air Force. His unit flew twenty-nine sorties, doing their part to save the world from the heinous crimes of an evil dictator intent on purging the world of Jews, homosexuals, gypsies, Catholics, disabled people, psychiatric patients, and anyone else Hitler deemed undesirable. Dad witnessed things during the war that he spent the rest of his life trying to forget.

He retired just before our son, Michael, was born. Soon after Michael's birth, he and Ann began a Wednesday routine of spending the day with their grandson. Three years later, our daughter, Stacey, was born and they continued the commitment.

Each year when I renewed the subscription to our favorite Christian publication, I included a second subscription for my in-laws. It wasn't an in-your-face magazine, just some inspirational stories written by regular people finding hope from a loving God. After the fourth year or so of these subscriptions, Dad confessed, "Suzy, thank you for the subscriptions, but you don't need to spend your money on that crap. I'm not gonna read it." And so I stopped.

One time, to my surprise, he informed me that many years earlier he had read the Bible cover to cover—twice. "Really?" I asked him, "and you're not convinced God is a loving Father?"

"Well, I've seen a lot of terrible things in my life. What happened during the war ... I can hardly bear to think of it. I just don't know how God could allow such evil to play out."

Years later, dear Dad began a slow decline from age-related illnesses. During the months of his suffering, my husband, then a newly committed Christian, often visited his father's bedside. He told him in little snippets about the love of God the Father and the sacrifice of Jesus on the cross for the forgiveness of the sins of all believers. Dad just listened.

On one of my visits, I asked Dad if I could pray for him. He nodded. I put my hand on the shoulder of the man I had grown to love so deeply over the previous three decades, and I began to pray aloud. I thanked God for Dad's kindness. I asked God to open his heart, to comfort him and to make his pain bearable. I asked that he would feel Jesus beside him in his time of suffering. After about two minutes of prayer, Dad, in his faint, weakened voice said to me, "Okay, that's enough." Now *that* was funny. He had welcomed the prayer, but his tolerance for my verbal crooning had its limits.

Despite cutting me short, he remained open to hearing about God's love. So during our many visits, my husband and I told him how much we loved him and how much God loved him too.

In his waning days, we were still unsure if he had turned to God, although he seemed to be softening. Eventually, he was no longer able to speak. On his last day of life, we sat at his bedside. Steve held his left hand and I held his right one. "Dad, I want to ask you about something and please tell me truthfully. Do you believe Jesus loves you? Do you believe He died for your sins and is waiting for you? Squeeze my hand if the answer is yes." He squeezed not only my hand, but Steve's hand as well.

It was then we knew Dad could go. But we also knew he was troubled about leaving his son and grandchildren behind.

"You can go, Dad," said Steve. "I'll be okay."

"You can go, Grandpa. I'll be all right," said Michael.

And Stacey assured him as well. "I'll be okay, Grandpa. You can go." And very soon, he did go.

Just as Jesus suffered alongside the criminal on the cross, Jesus suffered alongside my father-in-law at the end of his life. Scripture is resplendent with examples and proclamations of the relentless love of the Father and of Jesus, His Son.

God will not let one of us go until He has done everything possible to turn our hearts toward Him. So great is His love for us that He sacrificed His only son to suffer on our behalf so the debt of our sins could be paid and forgiveness extended. We are afforded a choice. Live with God or live apart from Him. The decision we make in this life follows us to the next.

Some choose to follow Jesus. Some do not. All are sinful. No sin is too grievous, no hour too late to accept the sacrifice of a Savior whose love is so great that He suffered heinous agony on our behalf, and in the midst of His own suffering proclaimed, "Truly I tell you, today you will be with me in paradise."

You, Lord, are forgiving and good, abounding in love to all who call to you.
Psalm 86:5

Can You Relate?

Questions for Personal Reflection or Group Discussion

1. Jesus intently carried out a pre-determined plan for the last three years before His death. What was His objective for those final years of His earthly life?

   _____

   _____

2. The sins of each of the criminals hanging beside Jesus were similar. What do you think caused one to repent while the other died in his sin?

   _____

   _____

3. Do you know anyone who made the decision to follow Jesus late in life? What were the circumstances?

   _____

   _____

4. Do you think it's fair that someone who lives a life of sin, shunning God, can turn toward Him late in life and spend eternity in heaven?

   _____

   _____

5. Which of Jesus' actions in the last week of His life strike you as poignant or impressive?

   _____

   _____

CHAPTER 9

ᘓᘛᐤᘚᘔ

Jesus Travels with the Disciples on the Emmaus Road

Now that same day two of them were going to a village called Emmaus, about seven miles from Jerusalem. They were talking with each other about everything that had happened. As they talked and discussed these things with each other, Jesus himself came up and walked along with them; but they were kept from recognizing him.

He asked them, "What are you discussing together as you walk along?"

They stood still, their faces downcast. One of them, named Cleopas, asked him, "Are you the only one visiting Jerusalem who does not know the things that have happened there in these days?"

"What things?" he asked.

"About Jesus of Nazareth," they replied. "He was a prophet, powerful in word and deed before God and all the people. The chief priests and our rulers handed him over to be sentenced to death, and they crucified him; but we had hoped that he was the

one who was going to redeem Israel. And what is more, it is the third day since all this took place. In addition, some of our women amazed us. They went to the tomb early this morning but didn't find his body. They came and told us that they had seen a vision of angels, who said he was alive. Then some of our companions went to the tomb and found it just as the women had said, but they did not see Jesus."

He said to them, "How foolish you are, and how slow to believe all that the prophets have spoken! Did not the Messiah have to suffer these things and then enter his glory?" And beginning with Moses and all the Prophets, he explained to them what was said in all the Scriptures concerning himself.

As they approached the village to which they were going, Jesus continued on as if he were going farther. But they urged him strongly, "Stay with us, for it is nearly evening; the day is almost over." So he went in to stay with them.

When he was at the table with them, he took bread, gave thanks, broke it and began to give it to them. Then their eyes were opened and they recognized him, and he disappeared from their sight. They asked each other, "Were not our hearts burning within us while he talked with us on the road and opened the Scriptures to us?"

Luke 24:13-35

Clarity for the Confused

It was time to go home. Like throngs of other Jews, Cleopas and his companion had made the trip to Jerusalem a week earlier. Able-bodied Jews came from all corners of the Palestinian region to Jerusalem, home of the holy temple for a weeklong celebration of God's love and constant provision.

For Cleopas and his companion, the trip was short, just a two-hour walk down the dusty road. They had expected this year's trek to be like those of years past: a week of reuniting with friends and loved ones, kibitzing at the temple, and reflecting on God's endless mercy. But this year's Passover summit had not been like the others. Nobody had anticipated the things that had taken place in the Holy City this year.

The festivities began with an impromptu parade that featured only one attraction: Jesus of Nazareth. He hadn't been seen for a while—not since He had raised His friend Lazarus, who had been dead for four days, with the simple command, "Lazarus, come out!"[33] Many people had speculated that Jesus was the Messiah promised by God to save His people. But Lazarus's resurrection had convinced them. The eyewitnesses told others what had happened, and the word traveled with the force of a tsunami: Jesus was indeed the Messiah. He would save them!

When Jesus entered the city on the back of a donkey, a vast crowd rushed out to meet Him. Many lined the road with their own cloaks, an honor extended to royalty. Other admirers cut palm branches from nearby trees and lined the path. The thunderous cry of "Hosanna!" reverberated through the city. The word is a shout of praise, which means "save." The crowd was welcoming the Messiah, the long-awaited Savior.

The excitement permeated the Passover crowd. "The Messiah is here!" they proclaimed, assuming they would be delivered from Roman rule and the city would be handed over to Jewish jurisdiction. The Scriptures had been consistent and clear: a savior would deliver the people, and they envisioned a messiah of the military variety.

But God had bigger plans.

When Jesus entered the temple area, the people soon saw evidence of the type of military leader they had been expecting. As prescribed by Jewish Law, a Passover offering was required. Each family was to sacrifice an unblemished lamb to God as a burnt offering. It reminded them that they were dependent on God for every provision, that God had always provided every need and would continue to do so. There was no reason to cling to what they had been given. God, in His benevolence, would continue to supply their daily needs.

But through the centuries, the simple idea of sacrifice had become complicated. The religious leaders had convoluted it into a set of burdensome rules: in order to gain God's approval, such-and-such was required. You could *earn* your way to God's favor, they said. For starters, there's no need to lug your offering with you from your homeland; you can buy your animal right here. We've set up a marketplace right inside the formerly holy temple grounds. Bring whatever currency you have from your hometown. We have a currency exchange right on the premises. Oh sure, there's a slight markup for the merchandise. Consider it a convenience fee. The load on your trip will be lighter. Our pockets will be heavier. Win-win.

When Jesus witnessed the desecration of the temple, He was filled with righteous indignation. He began driving out those who were buying and selling there. He overturned the tables of the moneychangers and the benches of those selling doves. Quoting prophecy from Jewish Scripture, He exposed their sin. "Is it not written: 'My house will be called a house of prayer for all nations'? But you have made it 'a den of robbers'."[34]

By quoting that Scripture, Jesus declared that the pious religious leaders were actually fulfilling prophecies spoken by Jeremiah six hundred years earlier. Their acts were detestable to God.

Jesus spent the week teaching in the temple courts. He told His followers what they should do after He was gone. He gave them a final example of how to love, how to serve. On Thursday He celebrated the solemn Passover meal with His twelve closest friends. One of them betrayed Jesus to the religious leaders for thirty pieces of silver, the standard price for a slave.[35]

Jesus was the silent defendant in a mock trial. Although the Roman authorities could find no fault with Him, they turned Jesus over to a Roman centurion to be crucified because they feared their own political standing would otherwise be threatened. Jesus was then subjected to brutal beatings no animal should ever have to endure. He was then crucified—nailed to a tree. It was the cruelest, darkest form of capital punishment, reserved for the vilest of criminals.

Cleopas and his companion had been among the hundreds of thousands that had witnessed Jesus' death. No, it hadn't been a typical Passover week. Their hearts were broken and their hopes were crushed. *We had hoped He was the one who was going to redeem Israel. How could we have been so wrong? Where is God?*

And then on Sunday morning, the third day, they were

astonished at the report that the battered body of their beloved Jesus, which had been placed in a guarded tomb, was missing. The women who had gone to the tomb had seen a vision of angels. And one of the angels had said Jesus was alive. Alive. Three days dead and now ... alive? How could it be? It was all too much to comprehend.

It was time to go home.

So Cleopas and his companion began their journey. As they walked along the road, they lamented to one another: "What will we do now? Who will save our people?" They were sickened by the images that replayed in their minds—images of a bloodied Jesus hanging on a tree as insults were hurled at Him, and images of an empty tomb but no sign of Jesus or His corpse.

And then a stranger joined them on the road. He asked them what they were discussing. They did not recognize Jesus, so they bemoaned to the stranger all that had happened. Jesus responded with words that clarified all that had occurred. The man they had seen crucified, He told them, was indeed the Messiah that God had promised. Jesus explained the many prophecies that had been written about Him over the previous fourteen centuries, concluding with how He must die for the sins of many, but that He would be raised from the dead on the third day.

When they arrived home, Cleopas and his companion implored Jesus to stay for a meal. Jesus accepted their invitation. When Jesus broke the bread, giving thanks to the loving Father as He had always done, they recognized Jesus. And then He was gone.

On the road, they hadn't recognized Jesus—not by sight. But their hearts had recognized Him: "Were not our hearts burning within us while He talked with us on the road and opened the Scriptures to us?"

When I was a very young girl, there was no Bible in our home. My parents were kind and morally upstanding. They told us that we were Christians, which meant we believed Jesus died on the cross for our sins. *Okay,* I thought. *I'm a Christian.* That seemed fine with me.

My parents made sure we kids went to Sunday services at our local church, and each year they enrolled us in religious education classes. The church we attended had a standard worship service format that included a brief reading of Scripture followed by a sermon. I don't remember anything about a single sermon I heard when I was a child. The boring services were far too structured and subdued for my boisterous personality. As the lines of church members paraded up and down the aisles to receive communion, I knelt with my hands folded and eyes turned downward, evaluating the relative attractiveness of the shoes that passed. *I love that pair! I wonder where she got them … Yikes! Look at the bunions on her feet … Whoa! What was she thinking when she bought those?*

I did more than critique shoes and feet, though. The artwork in our church depicted Jesus' suffering: stumbling as He struggled to bear the heavy wooden cross; blood trickling down His face from the beatings He had endured and from the crown of thorns pressed onto His head; his lacerated back, red and raw from merciless whippings. And there were also statues. The one that impacted me most powerfully was the one of Mary, holding the crucified body of her cherished son.

In Sunday school class, I was told that Jesus was God's Son and that He had endured all of the torture to pay for everyone's sins, including mine. I didn't understand it very well, but at some level I believed it was true. I felt indebted to God and to this Jesus I didn't know much about and could not understand. In gratitude, I vowed to "try to be good."

When I was ten or so, something very important happened. The doorbell rang, and when Mom answered it, a Bible salesman stood on our porch. My mother told us that the salesman asked her if she knew what was inscribed on Jesus' cross. She knew—"Jesus of Nazareth, the King of the Jews"—and so she won the Bible. I suspect maybe she won the "basic" model of the Bible and paid extra to upgrade. The Bible she placed on our coffee table was ornate, with a gold-colored cover and filigree edges. The center was filled with about twenty pages of religious art. I gazed at those pictures for hours.

Other than its artwork, though, the book intimidated me. It was so big. As an average ten-year-old reader, I never attempted to read it. So I just stuck with the artwork.

A couple of years later, I decided to begin with the New Testament—the part that talked about Jesus' earthly life. I read the first book, Matthew, and was captivated. There was so much I didn't understand, though. I asked Mom a few questions, but her biblical knowledge was limited. I didn't know anybody who knew much about Jesus or Christianity, so my questions remained unanswered. But I did know this: when I read the Scriptures, my heart burned within me.

In the days that followed Jesus' resurrection, He appeared to more than five hundred people. He met several times with His disciples and His closest followers. He told them that He would return to heaven to be with His Father, but that He would send the Holy Spirit, who would live inside all believers and be their Comforter, Counselor, and Guide. He then ascended to heaven and was seen no more.

Two thousand years have passed. Those who sought and carried out Jesus' death sentence thought they were finally rid of the thorn in their sides. They had no idea. The followers who had witnessed His life, death, and resurrection—the former glory-seekers, those who tried to turn the children away from Jesus, the disciple who denied he even knew Jesus, the former tax collector—the whole band of them began a movement that forever changed the world. Each was willing to die a martyr's death by governmental proclamation rather than to obey orders that forbade them from spreading word of the risen Christ. They had seen Him with their own eyes and could not deny it, no matter the consequences.

Early in the movement, the religious leaders discussed what to do about Jesus' annoying followers. Gamaliel, a respected teacher of Jewish Law, advised them to leave the men alone. "For if their purpose or activity is of human origin, it will fail. But if it is from God, you will not be able to stop these men; you will only find yourselves fighting against God."[36]

That is precisely what happened. The persecutors of those who followed Jesus were fighting against God. They could execute the leaders of the revolution—and they did. In AD 64, Nero instituted the first government-sanctioned persecutions of Christians.[37] Under his rule, both Peter and Paul were executed.

In the first three centuries after Jesus' resurrection, the Romans continued to subject Christians to periodic persecution. Executions were astonishingly cruel. Among the methods used to kill them were death by fire-at-the-stake, beheading, crucifixion, stretching them until their limbs were ripped from their torsos, and feeding them to lions. The executions were usually held in public places because the Romans hoped to deter other Christians from practicing and proclaiming their faith. Historians estimate almost one thousand Christians were executed during that time. Many others were tortured, but their lives spared. These people accepted torture and the cruelest of deaths rather than deny their love and devotion to their Savior, who had also died in agony because of His great love for all people. The Roman rulers thought those acts of cruelty would squash the Christian movement. Instead, the calm manner in which the early believers endured such torment made onlookers wonder why the Christians would bear such agony rather than denounce Jesus. Instead of crushing the movement, Jesus' church gained momentum.

Christian persecution continues. Although much of the world enjoys freedom of religion, Christians are still persecuted in many parts of the world and remain the most persecuted religious group. Today, over 200 million Christians in at least fifty countries are denied fundamental human rights solely because of their faith. Such persecution occurs in North Korea, Saudi Arabia, Afghanistan, Iraq, Somalia, and many other countries.[38] Despite the continued persecution, about one-third of the world's population professes to be Christian.[39] As Gamaliel said, "If it is from God, you will not be able to stop these men. You will only find yourself fighting against God."

Christianity is not about numbers. And of those professing to be Christians, surely there are those who do not enjoy a real bond with the risen Christ. But two thousand years after His death, the Church founded on the crucified carpenter from Nazareth still stands.

And why does it continue to stand? Is it because of the theological dissertations of learned men? Is it spurred by intellectual persuasion that the leader of the band of twelve disciples is truly the Son of God? Theological books and debates are beneficial. But they do not convince a person to center his life on a historical figure who lived and died centuries ago.

Jesus continues to change the world one soul at a time for one reason only: when He walks with us and we hear Him speak, our hearts burn within us.

And hope does not put us to shame, because God's love has been poured out into our hearts through the Holy Spirit, who has been given to us.
Romans 5:5

Can You Relate?

Questions for Personal Reflection or Group Discussion

1. Share, if you choose, your first introduction to Jesus, the Bible, or Christian principles.

   _____

   _____

2. Why do you think Cleopas and his companion failed to recognize Jesus as they walked with Him to Emmaus?

   _____

   _____

3. Have you ever read any Scripture or literature about the life of Christ and felt your heart burn within you? If so, what do you think generated that sensation?

   _____

   _____

4. Sue's life has been profoundly affected by religious art. Have you ever been moved by religious art or music?

   _____

   _____

5. The religious leaders thought they had rid themselves of Jesus and His mission once they had executed Him. Two thousand years later, the church He founded still stands, and His words continue to burn in the hearts of men and women, boys and girls, throughout the world. How do you explain that?

   _____

   _____

CHAPTER 10

Jesus Meets with
Nicodemus at Night

There was a man named Nicodemus, a Jewish religious leader who was a Pharisee. After dark one evening, he came to speak with Jesus. "Rabbi," he said, "we all know that God has sent you to teach us. Your miraculous signs are evidence that God is with you."

Jesus replied, "I tell you the truth, unless you are born again, you cannot see the Kingdom of God."

"What do you mean?" exclaimed Nicodemus. "How can an old man go back into his mother's womb and be born again?"

Jesus replied, "I assure you, no one can enter the Kingdom of God without being born of water and the Spirit. Humans can reproduce only human life, but the Holy Spirit gives birth to spiritual life. So don't be surprised when I say, 'You must be born again.' The wind blows wherever it wants. Just as you can hear the wind but can't tell where it comes from or where it is going, so you can't explain how people are born of the Spirit."

"How are these things possible?" Nicodemus asked.

Jesus replied, "You are a respected Jewish teacher, and yet you don't understand these things? I assure you, we tell you what we know and have seen, and yet you won't believe our testimony. But if you don't believe me when I tell you about earthly things, how can you possibly believe if I tell you about heavenly things? No one has ever gone to heaven and returned. But the Son of Man has come down from heaven. And as Moses lifted up the bronze snake on a pole in the wilderness, so the Son of Man must be lifted up, so that everyone who believes in him will have eternal life.

"For God loved the world so much that he gave his one and only Son, so that everyone who believes in him will not perish but have eternal life. God sent his Son into the world not to judge the world, but to save the world through him.

"There is no judgment against anyone who believes in him. But anyone who does not believe in him has already been judged for not believing in God's one and only Son. And the judgment is based on this fact: God's light came into the world, but people loved the darkness more than the light, for their actions were evil. All who do evil hate the light and refuse to go near it for fear their sins will be exposed. But those who do what is right come to the light so others can see that they are doing what God wants."

John 3:1-21(NLT)

Doorway of Deliverance

He had it all figured out.

As a Pharisee, Nicodemus had prided himself on his knowledge of Jewish Law. He had studied it since he was a young boy and had learned it well. Because of his zeal, he had eventually risen to a highly esteemed leadership and teaching position. He and his buddies were proud of their many good works. They were respected for the generous offerings they gave at the temple. In the marketplace, everyone knew Nicodemus and greeted him with the high title of "Rabbi." He was acknowledged with a place of honor whenever he attended a wedding or a banquet. Nicodemus and his friends were assigned the most important seats in the synagogues. Cool stuff. *It's good to be me*, Nicodemus had often thought.

Nicodemus took particular pride in his ability to teach at the temple and to interpret Scripture in a way that the common Jews could not. They sought his counsel because he had figured it all out long ago.

But then a carpenter from the low-class town of Nazareth in the region of Galilee had begun to teach at the synagogues throughout Judea. Nicodemus had taken note of Jesus' profound teachings. Indeed, it would have been impossible not to notice. The crowds flocked to Him wherever He appeared. Not only was He teaching with authority and profundity, He was also performing acts that could only be described as miraculous. And by definition, since He was performing miracles, He must therefore have been sent by God Himself.

So *all* were taking note, including the Pharisees and teachers of the Jewish Law. They had discussed it amongst themselves. Jesus was certainly intriguing. The Pharisees often quizzed Jesus at the synagogues or at the temple to see whether He really knew what He was talking about. They were not ready to invite Him into the fold, though. At that point, they had kept Him at arm's length.

Nicodemus couldn't deny the miraculous signs Jesus had performed. He had talked about it with some of his friends. They also admitted Jesus was a teacher sent from God Himself.

Unlike his friends, Nicodemus humbled himself to seek out Jesus. He decided to pay Him a personal visit so he could learn more about this man of God. He came to see Jesus after dark so they could have a private conversation without the crowds pressing in. Maybe they could have an intellectual discussion about Scripture or the nature of God. Nicodemus felt sure Jesus could provide some profound insight.

Nicodemus quickly acknowledged that he and his colleagues believed Jesus had been sent by God to teach them. Unfortunately, most of the Pharisees would later do an about-face on their position and demand that Jesus be executed. But not Nicodemus.

So in the initial face-to-face, one-on-one meeting with the Master, Nicodemus came with a teachable heart. Jesus quickly discerned the Pharisee's problem and let him know straightaway. Nicodemus had all the book learning a man could possibly need. But in order to see the kingdom of God—the perfect kingdom God designed—he would need a spiritual rebirth. "Unless you are born again, Nicodemus, you cannot see the Kingdom of God," Jesus said.

Nicodemus was flummoxed by Jesus' statement. He thought

Jesus was referring to a physical rebirth and asked, "How can an old man go back into his mother's womb and be born again?"

Jesus explained to Nicodemus the difference between a physical birth and a spiritual birth. He said that there are things in this world we cannot fully understand. You can hear the wind but don't know the nature of it. Likewise, you can't explain how people are spiritually born. But Nicodemus still didn't get it. Why? Because he had only book knowledge. He hadn't been born again.

Jesus then told Nicodemus that, as a respected teacher, he should have known such things. But Jesus' proclamation still made no sense to Nicodemus.

Jesus reminded Nicodemus about something profound that had happened to the Jewish people in ancient times. The story was certainly familiar to Nicodemus. The Jews had rebelled against God and had to be punished. God sent fiery serpents that bit the people and infected them with lethal venom. But God is gracious and takes no pleasure in the death of the wicked. Scripture says He wants them instead to turn from their wicked ways and live. To save the people from death, God provided a remedy. He told Moses to make a brass serpent and lift it up on a pole for all to see. In that way, God would dispense His grace. Any stricken person who gazed upon the serpent, He told Moses, would immediately be healed. Moses relayed the information to those who had been afflicted. If they had no faith, then they would consider the antidote ridiculous. They would refuse to look upon the raised pole, and they would die in their sin. But if they had faith, they would do as Moses instructed them. They would look upon the raised pole and they would live, as was God's desire.[40] Metaphorically, it would be the same with him, Jesus told Nicodemus. "The Son of Man must be lifted up, so that everyone who believes in Him will have eternal life." Jesus was foretelling His impending death and resurrection. But Nicodemus had not been born again. And he did not understand.

Jesus explained why it would be as He had said: "For God loved the world so much that he gave his one and only Son, so that everyone who believes in him will not perish but have eternal life." Then Jesus added God's purpose for sending Him: "God sent his Son into the world not to judge the world, but to save the world through him."

Nicodemus, the highly respected teacher of the Law, became a student that day. He did not interject any wisdom or try to impress. Nicodemus walked away from Jesus into the dark of the night. He didn't fully understand what Jesus had told him. But he knew it was something big.

They were too young to understand. That much I knew. But it was important and I insisted they be there.

Steve and I married young. I was twenty. He had just turned twenty-two. I had just completed two years of college. My mom would have preferred that we wait until I graduated. But we had been together for almost four years, and we were in love. So on a beautiful day in June, I married the man who remains the love of my life.

Along with the marriage certificate came a starter home that we adored but that required lots of time and material for renovation. We also had all of the financial responsibilities most adults have: a mortgage, utilities, healthcare, clothing expenses, and on and on.

So ended my full-time college education. Over the next seven years, I worked full time and took one class per semester in the evenings. Along the way I changed majors—twice—forfeiting credits that would no longer be counted in the new degree program. When the kids came along, I put my college education on the back burner. For the next six years, working full time while raising two rambunctious kids consumed all of my time.

Still, I had the nagging desire to finish my college education. I wanted to graduate for three reasons. First, if I graduated, I thought I'd be able to get a job with greater schedule flexibility. I wanted to spend more time with my kids, and with a college degree, more options would be available to me. Second, I felt as if something important had been left incomplete, and I craved the satisfaction of finishing what I'd worked so many years to accomplish. Third, I wanted my mom to see me graduate.

So I headed back to college. The following eighteen months were mentally and physically exhausting—full-time work during the day, one night a week at school, and all the fun and responsibilities that come with having young kids. Then two hours of study every night after the kids were sound asleep. That's something that *I* didn't get much of during that time—sleep.

Still, it was a good experience. During the time I went to school, Steve immersed himself in daddy activities and developed a closer relationship with the kids. I formed kinships with the working adults in my classes. I felt a sense of satisfaction as I worked hard for something that was important. Finally, it was finished.

Graduation was held early in June at an outdoor ceremony. As the date drew near, the weather forecast called for sunny and hot—in the mid-nineties. I shopped for new outfits for our kids.

My mother-in-law questioned the prudence of bringing the kids to the ceremony because they were still very young. Michael was almost seven and Stacey would soon turn four. "They won't understand what's going on," Mom told me, "and they'll be hot and bored."

"And sweaty," I added. "I *want* them to be hot and bored and sweaty. I know they won't understand any of the speeches. I know they'll barely be able to see me from where they'll be sitting. But they'll know they dressed up in new outfits, stood among a swarm of other hot, sweaty people, and watched something important happen. They won't really understand what's so significant about it, but they'll know it's something big. In time, they'll understand the importance of education and of working relentlessly for things that matter." So on that sweltering June day, Michael and Stacey sat in the crowd with their dad and grandparents and witnessed something big.

That was over twenty years ago. Recently I asked my kids—now young adults—whether they remembered my college graduation.

"I remember the pictures," Stacey told me. "I remember what you looked like." But she didn't remember dressing up in a new outfit or being hot, sweaty, and bored. She was too young.

But then I asked Michael what he remembered about it. "I remember being there. It was hot. There were a lot of people. I knew it was important."

"Did it impress upon you the importance of education? Of working hard for important things?"

"I was too young to process how I was feeling about it at the time," Michael said. "Since then, yes, you and Dad have always emphasized the importance of education and of working hard. At the time, though, I only knew that something important was going on."

Michael hadn't fully grasped the significance of my graduation at the time, but he knew it was important. He stored the memory in his heart and as he matured, he understood.

Two years had passed since Nicodemus first conversed with Jesus. A lot had happened.

Jesus had become increasingly critical of what the Pharisees had been doing. The Pharisees were hypocrites, He said. God had given His people commandments meant to protect and guide their hearts, but the Pharisees perverted the commandments into a set of outward rules of the road, designed to impress onlookers. The condition of the heart was of no concern to the Pharisees as long as the growing list of do's and don'ts was upheld.

"Do everything they tell you," Jesus told the crowds, "but do not do as they do, for they do not practice what they preach."[41] Furthermore, Jesus said the Pharisees were leading people *away from*, not toward, God by their distortion of God's holy decrees.

Is that me? Nicodemus wondered. *Have I been doing all the right things but neglecting justice and mercy? Have I left God out of this great set of laws that gives me good seats and high praise?*

"Blind guides!" Jesus called the Pharisees, because they carefully counted out one tenth of their earnings and displayed them on the altar, but they neglected the more important matters of the law—like justice, mercy, and faithfulness. "You strain out a gnat, but swallow a camel," Jesus said.[42]

He always had a way with words, thought Nicodemus. Words that penetrated stony hearts. Words of love. Words of conviction.

Yes, even the words of conviction were always spoken in love. Nicodemus recalled the words Jesus had spoken to him: "God didn't send His Son to condemn the world, but to save it."[43]

Somewhere along the way, Nicodemus reached the conclusion that most of the other Pharisees had vehemently resisted: Jesus was unequivocally right. The Pharisees focused on the superficial. They had neglected the work of God and led the people astray. Nicodemus knew in his heart that it was so. Jesus' words had illuminated Nicodemus's sin, and he was flooded with remorse.

Most of the other Pharisees dug in their heels, though. They stood firm in their conviction. *We sit in Moses' seat, and we'll make up our own rules, thank you.* They chose to continue in the direction they had invented, and they were determined to rally the people to their cause. "This Jesus must be stopped," they said. Then they set out to make it happen.

Nicodemus found himself in the middle of the plot.

Jesus was in Jerusalem for the Feast of the Tabernacles, one of three major feasts celebrated each year. Midway through the eight-day feast, Jesus began preaching in the temple courts. The Pharisees had been looking for an opportunity to arrest Him, and they sent a troop of temple guards to do so. The guards headed to the temple, but when they arrived, they heard Jesus addressing the people. Their hearts were pierced and they returned to the Pharisees.

"Why didn't you bring him in?" they demanded.

"No one ever spoke the way this man does," declared the guards.[44]

Then the chief priests and Pharisees ranted about Jesus being a Galilean. "No way could a prophet come from *there*," they seethed.[45] In fact, at least two prophets had come from Galilee, but the Pharisees couldn't be sidetracked by facts.[46] Their bigotry was surpassed only by their piety. They had convicted Jesus by consensus, even though they hadn't even queried Him about their yet-to-be-determined charges. Nor had they found witnesses to verify the charges.

Nicodemus disagreed and cited Jewish Law in his defense of Jesus. "Does our law condemn a man without first hearing him to find out what he has been doing?"[47] According to Jewish Law, even a common criminal was entitled to a trial with at least two concurring witnesses. Surely Jesus deserved the same.

"Are you from Galilee, too?" the other Pharisees asked Nicodemus.[48]

They had convicted Jesus already. And so, without Nicodemus's support, the religious leaders and Pharisees arranged for Jesus' arrest and put Him on trial.

Nicodemus was there to witness the travesty. He viewed the fake trial up close and personal. He had seen Jesus' "conviction" under Pontius Pilate, the Roman governor. He had a front seat when Jesus was punched and spit upon, then whipped and nailed to the cross. He saw the skin ripped from Jesus' back and His blood spilled out. He heard Jesus pray for the forgiveness of His tormenters and bestow salvation on the criminal hanging beside Him.

Then Nicodemus saw Jesus die.

No longer could the Pharisee be timid. It was time to defect. No longer stifled by fear, Nicodemus, along with his friend Joseph of Arimathea, went to Pilate and asked for permission to bury Jesus' body. A wealthy man, Nicodemus brought with him a mixture of myrrh and aloes. Using those spices and burial linens, he and Joseph prepared Jesus' body for entombment in accordance with Jewish Law. They had to hurry as it was getting late and the burial had to be completed before sunset. They laid Jesus' body in a nearby tomb and rolled the stone to seal it. [49]

Pilate then assigned guard detail at the tomb.

On the third day, Nicodemus heard the news.[50] The women had been to the tomb. The huge stone had been rolled away. They had seen a vision of angels, and one of them had told the women that Jesus was no longer among the dead. He was alive!

Hearing the words, Nicodemus again reflected upon the words Jesus had spoken to him in the night. "The Son of Man has come down from heaven. And as Moses lifted up the bronze snake on a pole in the wilderness, so the Son of Man must be lifted up, so that everyone who believes in him will have eternal life."

Yes, as the snake had been lifted up on the pole, Jesus had been lifted up on the cross. Nicodemus now understood that it had been a part of the plan all along. "For God loved the world so much," Jesus had told him, "that he gave his one and only Son so that anyone who believes in him will not perish but have eternal life."

Nicodemus hadn't understood those words when Jesus first spoke them, but now His words were as clear as polished crystal. Nicodemus's heart cried out, "I believe! To the depths of my soul, I believe" Nicodemus knew that he would have eternal life, just as Jesus promised, and that his earthly life would never be the same.

Humble yourselves before the Lord, and he will
lift you up.
James 4:10

Can You Relate?

Questions for Personal Reflection or Group Discussion

1. Scripture suggests that Nicodemus's devotion to Jesus progressed over time: First, he was intrigued by Jesus and sought to learn from Him. Next, he protested against Jesus' condemnation without benefit of a hearing. Finally, he petitioned the Roman governor for Jesus' body so he could honor Him with a dignified burial.

   a. Are you currently on a journey to know Jesus better?

   _____

   _____

   b. Do you have a story of gradual devotion to Jesus that you wish to share?

   _____

   _____

   c. Why do you think some people make instantaneous decisions to follow Jesus and others take considerable time before deciding to follow Him?

   _____

   _____

2. Most of the Pharisees never accepted Jesus. In fact, they plotted to carry out His execution. By contrast, Nicodemus became a follower of Jesus. What do you think was different about Nicodemus compared to most other Pharisees?

   _____

   _____

3. Do you think that intelligence and education are influences in deciding to follow Jesus, or do you think that the decision is equally easy to make regardless of these factors?

_____

_____

4. The Bible is not always easy to understand. Do you think it is necessary to have all your questions about Christianity answered before deciding to follow Jesus?

_____

_____

5. Share, if you choose, any reservations you have that prevent you from following Jesus.

_____

_____

6. Reflect upon your own messed upness and the love Jesus has for messed up people.

    a. What does that tell you about the nature of Jesus?

    _____

    _____

    b. Have these stories of Jesus' interactions with messed up people prompted any changes in your heart or in your attitude about Jesus?

    _____

    _____

EPILOGUE:

Grace Like Rain

It's been said that big things come in small packages, and such is often true. A young woman opens a velveteen box coyly presented by her beloved to reveal a sparkling diamond ring inside that is truly so much more than a ring. The gem represents a declaration of undying love. It marks the anticipation of an intimate union that will last through every season of their lives, however brief or long lasting … provided she says yes.

Fleeting snippets of time—brief encounters with Jesus. They all had them: the Samaritan woman at the well; the rich young man; Zacchaeus, the tax collector; the adulterous woman; Mary and her sister, Martha; the sinful woman with the alabaster jar; the two criminals hanging on the cross; Cleopas and his companion; Nicodemus, the Pharisee. Just snippets of time— small packages that held big things, bigger than the promise contained in a diamond ring. Each of those snippets had the power to mark the beginning of an intimate union with the Messiah of the universe … provided they said yes.

Saying yes to Jesus means making a choice to follow Him. That choice cannot be casual. Just as the young woman who accepts the diamond from her beloved commits to a lifetime of entwining her life with his, so must a follower of Jesus entwine their life with His. Jesus cannot be just a part of the life of the Christian; Jesus is the epicenter of the Christian's life. Saying yes means big changes lie ahead. It requires an extreme makeover of the heart.

Some said yes. Zacchaeus did. From the time he met Jesus, his heart was transformed. He left his life as tax-thief-for-hire and centered his life on the Savior who had cleansed his sooty soul, turning it snow white.

The sinful woman with the alabaster jar of perfume said yes. She left philandering behind and chose instead to love the Lord who had extended mercy to her.

Nicodemus said yes. That decision caused him to leave behind his high societal standing, turning away from the inferior manmade regulations that had been his foundation. Instead, he chose to lean on the grace Jesus offered.

The Samaritan woman at the well said yes to Jesus. She not only left her bucket at the well, she left her sad life of serial monogamy at the well too. Jesus' love spurred her to become his fervent advocate.

The adulterous woman said yes as well. Jesus didn't simply spare her life. He required her to leave her life of sin behind.

Kirsten and Scott Strand chose Jesus. They left their upscale lifestyle to live among the downtrodden. Their love for Jesus overflows and stirs in them a desire to love those who struggle to put food on the table and to provide simple Christmas gifts for their children.

Fred and Melissa said yes. They have devoted their lives and their resources to serve those in need.

Others said no. They declined the invitation of the Messiah who gave His own life so they might experience life to the full.

The rich young man went away sad, giving no indication that he could leave behind his wealth, the focal point of his life.

The defiant criminal hanging on the cross beside Jesus had turned his back on God, staunchly clinging to his illicit ways and refusing even in death to repent and follow the Messiah to paradise.

As a young girl, I meditated upon the statues that adorned our church. They stirred in me an intrigue about the man who loved greatly and suffered bitterly. Later, I contemplated the religious artwork in our family Bible, further stimulating my intrigue. Eventually, I began to read the Bible and was enthralled by what it said. Though my understanding was minimal, my heart burned as I read about the carpenter from Nazareth.

As far back as I can remember, it only made sense to me that since there was a creation, it logically followed that there must therefore be a creator. That creator must have pre-existed everything. Most people refer to that creator as God. I don't know how God created the universe and all that is in it, and I don't know how long it took. But as I behold the sparkle in my daughter's eyes and drink in her loving nature, I am convinced she was no cosmic accident. Gazing upon either of my children spurs in me an overwhelming desire to worship the Creator who has blessed me with them.

When my son, Michael, was a newborn, I spent long moments just marveling at his tiny hands, perfectly designed to serve him for a lifetime. With those hands, he would explore his ever-expanding world. Through the tactile sensitivity of those little hands, he would feel my love and the affection of all who were delighted with his arrival. He would use those hands to hold on to me, or his dad, until he was ready to navigate crossing streets. He would learn that roses are soft and silky and that worms are cool and slimy. He would learn that ice is cold and that the sidewalk is warm on a sunny day in June.

Once, when he was about two years old, Michael was contemplating his hands, and he made a splendid discovery. "Hey, I have roundies on my fingers!" he told us, having just discovered his fingerprints. Yes, God even thought of putting roundies on our fingers—and scientists tell us each person's fingerprints are as unique as the person bearing them.

One day, my son's fingers will intermingle intimately with the fingers of the woman God designed for him before either of them was formed in their mother's womb. And one day their hands will likely hold their own baby, and they too will marvel at what God has wonderfully created.

My marvel of creation goes far beyond hands and fingerprints. I look at my dog, curled up in my lap and gazing lovingly into my eyes. I cannot imagine why dogs would exist if not for a Creator who loves people … and dogs.

Birds sing. Why would they do that if not for a Creator who knows that the sound would be lovely?

I see trees and flowers, clouds and stars. I ponder the awesome design of the sun that could never support life were it just a bit smaller or larger, or just a bit closer or farther.

For a long while, I attempted to figure out the nature of the Creator on my own. Turns out that God has not blessed me with omniscience, though, so I eventually learned that I needed to turn to another source—the Bible. People far more learned than I have found it to be highly reliable.

The Bible was written during a time span of about 1500 years. It is comprised of sixty-six books, written by thirty authors. Many of the authors of the Bible had no access to any other books that are contained in the Bible. Other authors had read some of the other books and in their writings offer commentary on those books. There is astonishing consistency between the books.

The theme of the Bible is simple. Its sixty-six books, now compiled into one collection, tell the story of God's love for His people and His relentless pursuit of their hearts.

Jewish Scriptures, which Christians call the Old Testament, contain dozens of stunning prophecies about the Messiah that God promised to send. Only Jesus matches the prophecies recorded centuries before He was born in Bethlehem. Seven hundred years before Jesus walked the earth, the prophet Isaiah recorded these words:

> He was despised and rejected by mankind, a man of suffering, and familiar with pain.
>
> Like one from whom people hide their faces he was despised, and we held him in low esteem.
>
> Surely he took up our pain and bore our suffering, yet we considered him punished by God, stricken by him, and afflicted.
>
> But he was pierced for our transgressions, he was crushed for our iniquities; the punishment that brought us peace was on him, and by his wounds we are healed.
>
> We all, like sheep, have gone astray, each of us has turned to our own way; and the LORD has laid on

him the iniquity of us all.

He was oppressed and afflicted, yet he did not open his mouth; he was led like a lamb to the slaughter, and as a sheep before its shearers is silent, so he did not open his mouth.

By oppression and judgment he was taken away . . .

He was assigned a grave with the wicked, and with the rich in his death, though he had done no violence, nor was any deceit in his mouth …

For he bore the sin of many, and made intercession for the transgressors.[51]

The prophecies point repeatedly to Jesus, and the pages of the New Testament tell the rich stories of His walk on earth. When I read those stories, my heart burns within me.

Jesus said God loves each of us so wildly and so personally that He invites us to call Him *Abba*, an Aramaic translation of Father, expressing an intimate relationship. Jesus further explained that our loving, perfect, sinless Father cannot tolerate any sin. Sin separates us from a perfect, untainted God. All people do sin, though, and each of us deserves to pay the penalty for our sins. That penalty is death.

But the prophets foretold, and Jesus confirmed, that God had a grand plan. Rather than confer the death penalty on sinful people, God decided to send a proxy to receive the punishment we deserve. In willing submission to the Father, Jesus endured that punishment, pouring down grace like rain on all who would simply acknowledge His sacrifice on their behalf. Jesus said that those who choose to follow Him become heirs to the kingdom of God. That kingdom begins in this life and follows us to eternal life.

"For God loved the world so much," Jesus said, "that he gave his one and only Son, so that everyone who believes in him will not perish but have eternal life. God sent his Son into the world not to judge the world, but to save the world through him. There is no judgment against anyone who believes in him. But anyone who does not believe in him has already been judged for not believing in God's one and only Son. And the judgment is based on this fact: God's light came into the world, but people loved the darkness more than the light, for their actions were evil."[52]

Each person has a choice to make on the Jesus question— He told us this Himself. Either He was and is who He claimed to be or He is not. And there is absolutely no question of who He said He was. He said He could forgive sin. He said that no one comes to the Father except through Him. He said He was God. Jesus consistently made all these claims and He was killed for it.

C. S. Lewis, British atheist turned Christian, and one of the most brilliant minds of the twentieth century put it this way:

> I am trying here to prevent anyone from saying
> the really foolish thing that people often say about
> Him: "I'm ready to accept Jesus as a great moral
> teacher, but I don't accept his claim to be God."
> That is the one thing we must not say. A man who
> was merely a man and said the sort of things Jesus
> said would not be a great moral teacher. He would
> either be a lunatic—on the level with the man who
> says he is a poached egg—or else he would be the

Devil of Hell. You must make your choice. Either this man was, and is, the Son of God, or else a madman or something worse. You can shut him up for a fool, you can spit at him and kill him as a demon: or you can fall at his feet and call him Lord and God. But let us not come with any patronising nonsense about his being a great human teacher. He has not left that open to us. He did not intend to ... Now it seems to me obvious that He was neither a lunatic nor a fiend: and consequently, however strange or terrifying or unlikely it may seem, I have to accept the view that He was and is God.[53]

They each had to choose. Each and every messed up one of them: Nicodemus, the woman at the well, Zacchaeus, the adulterous woman, Martha, Mary, the woman with the alabaster jar, Simon, the criminals hanging beside Jesus, Cleopas and his companion, and the wealthy man who wanted to inherit eternal life.

Jesus loved each of them just as they were. He came to each one and gave them a choice. So great is His love for all people that He comes to each of us—just as we are—and we, likewise, must choose.

I choose Jesus.

AUTHOR'S NOTE

I hope you enjoyed *Messiah to the Messed Up*. If so, I would be grateful if you wrote a brief review on Amazon. Reviews are tremendously helpful to authors. I would love to hear from you too. Please connect with me at sueciullo.com

LINKS THAT I LOVE

Find answers to your faith questions:
http://www.leestrobel.com/

Find a church near you:
- NewThing Network churches are relentlessly dedicated to helping people find their way back to God http://www.newthing.org
- Community Christian Church provides links to recent video messages. http://communitychristian.org/

North Point Ministries makes available, for free, a myriad of intriguing, stirring videos, exploring Christian beliefs. http://www.youtube.com/user/northpointministries

Bible Gateway is a free, searchable online Bible, offering multiple Bible translations. http://www.biblegateway.com

Endnotes

Chapter 1: : Jesus Talks with the Woman at the Well

[1] Easton, Matthew George. *The Illustrated Bible Dictionary*. Third edition. Nashville: Thomas Nelson, 1997. "Samaritans."

[2] Marshall, Howard, A. R. Millard, J. I. Packer, and Donald J. Wiseman. *The New Bible Dictionary*. Third Edition. Westmont, IL: Intervarsity Press, 1996. "Samaritans." p. 1052.

Chapter 2: Jesus Teaches the Disciples about Humility

[3] Matthew 5:3-5, 8, 10

[4] David Rubenstein. Personal Conversation. April 2012.

Chapter 3: Jesus Challenges the Rich Young Man

[5] Matthew 14:13

[6] Matthew 18:2-3

[7] Wiersbe, Warren W. *The Bible Exposition Commentary*. Colorado Springs: David C. Cook, 2007. Libronix DSL Electronic Edition. " Mark 10:17-31."

[8] Luke 10:1

[9] Luke 9:59-60

[10] Luke 9:61-62

Chapter 4: Jesus Protects the Adulterous Woman

[11] St. Augustine. *The Confessions of St. Augustine*. Translated into English, with an Introduction and Notes by John K. Ryan. New York: Image Books, 1960.

[12] Achtemeier, Paul. *Harper's Bible Dictionary*. General edition. New York: Harper and Row, 1985. "Adultery," p. 13

Chapter 5: Jesus Dines with Zacchaeus

[13] Achtemeier, Paul. *Harper's Bible Dictionary.* General edition. New York: Harper and Row, 1985. "Publicans," p. 841.

[14] Marshall, Howard, A. R. Millard, J. I. Packer, and Donald J. Wiseman. *The New Bible Dictionary.* Third Edition. Westmont, IL: Intervarsity Press, 1996. "New Testament Jericho," p. 556.

[15] Matthew 9:11

[16] Luke 5:31-32

[17] Luke 18:9-14

[18] Achtemeier, Paul. *Harper's Bible Dictionary.* General edition. New York: Harper and Row, 1985. "Sycamore," p. 1003

[19] Easton, Matthew George. *The Illustrated Bible Dictionary.* Third edition. Nashville: Thomas Nelson, 1997. "Salvation."

[20] Genesis 12:1-3

Chapter 6: Jesus Visits Martha and Mary

[21] John 11:5

[22] "At This Moment." Billy Vera. Recorded by Billy Vera and the Beaters. *Hopeless Romantic: The Best of Billy Vera and the Beaters.* Shout Factory Records, 2008.

Chapter 7: Jesus Defends a Sinful Woman

[23] 1 Corinthians 13:1-8, 13

[24] Luke 7:36, Luke 11:37, and Luke 14:1

[25] Walvoord, John F. and Roy B. Zuck. *The Bible Knowledge Commentary of the Scriptures by Dallas Theological Seminary.* Libronix DSL Electronic Edition. "Luke 7:36-38."

[26] Wiersbe, Warren W. *The Bible Exposition Commentary.* Colorado Springs: David C. Cook. 2007. Libronix DSL Electronic Edition. " Luke 7:36-38."

[27] Luke 6:21

Chapter 8: Jesus Forgives the Repentant Criminal

[28] John 13:5-17

[29] Matthew 26:38

[30] Matthew 26:39

[31] Wiersbe, Warren W. *The Bible Exposition Commentary.* Colorado Springs: David C. Cook. 2007. Libronix DSL Electronic Edition. "Luke 23:32-43."

[32] Ciullo, Gregory. Mike Ciullo's wake. 1 February 2002.

Chapter 9: Jesus Travels with the Disciples on the Emmaus Road

[33] John 11:1-44; 54-56

[34] Mark 11:17

[35] Exodus 21:32

[36] Acts 5:33-40, 38-39

[37] Tacitcus. *The Annals*. Kindle Edition, Acheron Press, 2012.

[38] Christian Reform Church. http://www2.crcna.org/pages/osj_crcandpersecution.cfm

[39] Pew Research Center. Global Christianity – A Report on the Size and Distribution of the World's Christian Population http://www.pewforum.org/2011/12/19/global-christianity-exec/

Chapter 10: Jesus Meets with Nicodemus at Night

[40] Numbers 21:4-9

[41] Matthew 23:3

[42] Matthew 23:24

[43] John 3:17 (NLT)

[44] John 7:45-46

[45] John 7:52

[46] Two prophets came from Galilee: Jonah was from Gath-heper and Elijah was from Thisbe. Both are in the Galilean Region. http://christiananswers.net/dictionary/galilee.html

[47] John 7:51

[48] John 7:52

[49] John 19:38-42

[50] Luke 24:9

Epilogue: Grace Like Rain

[51] Isaiah 53:3-9, 12

[52] John 3:16-19 (NLT)

[53] Lewis, C.S. *The Complete C. S. Lewis Signature Classics.* C.S. Lewis Pte. Ltd. Harper One edition.New York: Harper Collins Publishers, 2002. From *Mere Christianity*, pages 50-52.

34937888R00086

Made in the USA
Lexington, KY
24 August 2014